CREATING JUNIOR GENEALOGISTS

Creating Junior Genealogists

Tips and Activities for Family History Fun

Karen Frisch

Ancestry®

Library of Congress Cataloging-in-Publication Data

Frisch, Karen.
Creating junior genealogists : tips and activities for family history fun / by Karen Frisch.
p. cm.
Includes bibliographical references and index.
ISBN 1-59331-029-3 (alk. paper)
1. United States—Genealogy—Handbooks, manuals, etc. 2. Family recreation. 3. Creative activities and seat work. I. Title.

CS49.F74 2003
929'.1–dc22

2003023999

360 West 4800 North
Provo, UT 84604

10 9 8 7 6 5 4 3 2

Printed in Canada

To my daughters Elizabeth,
whose favorite bedtime story each night
used to always begin with the words,
"Once upon a time Mommy was in the woods,"
and Jennifer,
who loves books
as much as her mother does.

Acknowledgments

I'd like to thank everyone who has contributed to the completion of this book. Throughout its development I was privileged to talk with many people who inspired me in their dedication to their various genealogical efforts, some of whom were willing to share their stories with a total stranger.

Deepest thanks to Jo Ann Ferguson, Angela Healy, Lisa and Jim Mather, Elizabeth Wessen, Robyn and Richard Younkin, and Ed and Karen Dihrberg, my circle of friends and adoptive parents. They had the courage and commitment to address the joys of adoption and the challenges of identity issues. I'm indebted to Linda Lin, China Program Coordinator with Wide Horizons for Children, in Waltham, Massachusetts, for her help.

I'm also grateful to Ruth Thomasian of Project SAVE Armenian Photograph Archives, Inc., in Watertown, Massachusetts; David Lambert, library manager at New England Historic Genealogical Society in Boston; Claire V. Brisson-Banks, director of the LDS Family History Center in Warwick, Rhode Island; Patrick M. Leehey, Research Director at the Paul Revere Memorial Association in Boston; Jane Lancaster, Ph.D., of Providence, Rhode Island; Dr. Harold F. Worthley of Boston's Congregational Library; and Reverend Barry McCarthy, Pastor of Sayles Memorial Congregational Church, United Church of Christ in Lincoln, Rhode Island.

My eternal thanks to friends and relatives I depended upon for help: Dot Edgerton, Gail Brecher, Tim Bingham, Audrey Loberti, Gail Eastwood Stokes, Kim Salloway, Lois McDonald, Bill Brickel, Yan Li, Magdy Guirguis, John Glindeman, Heather Wasilewski, Anna

Haukness, Jennifer Gibson, Marcia Smith, Ph.D., Patti McAlpine, Anna Lindsey, Bonnie Cameron Laliberte, and Beverly Winger.

Very special thanks are extended to those who so agreeably came forward with information when asked: Sandra Cook, Kenelm C. Winslow, Daniel and Linda Hardman, Bob Buchanan, Lisa Murdough, Wayne Winters, Martha Marble, John and Beverly Clark, Wayne Winters, Margaret Palella, Frederick Stingle, Jr., Barbara Freshwater, Louise Albanese, Kathryn Edmonds, and Mary Allard.

I'd like to express my sincere appreciation and thanks to Loretto Dennis Szucs at Ancestry Publishing for helping to give this project wings and to Valerie Holladay for her faith in the book and patience with the writer. Also, my thanks to Jennifer Browning and all the editorial staff at Ancestry.

I especially thank my husband, Mark Dennen, for the gift of time. He provided insight and inspiration when mine quit.

I also owe a debt of gratitude to my many relatives, many of whom are no longer on this earth. Their tales have enriched my life and my memories.

Karen Frisch
Lincoln, Rhode Island

Table of Contents

Introduction

One day as I was wading through boxes of family history notes and photographs, it occurred to me that my daughters knew very little about their ancestors. So much of my genealogical research had been done before Beth and Jenny came into my life. They had missed the excitement of the discoveries I had made, the joy of finally identifying a certain lineage as belonging to my parents, and the anticipation as new clues led to more information.

I realized that I wanted to share with them the love I felt for my ancestors, the thrill of discovering who those ancestors were. I began to consider ways I might interest them in their family history and perhaps even help them to relive some of my discoveries and share some of the excitement I had felt. In this way, the idea for this book began to take shape in my mind.

As I talked with friends and fellow genealogists and tried various methods with my daughters, I came to the conclusion that several variables need to be in place before we can effectively introduce our children to their family history.

First, we need to know our ancestors and the world they lived in. We must be aware of the events of their lives and times, and the influences on them. If you are just beginning to research your family history, consider the stories you know and the historical perspective of your ancestors' lives.

Second, we need to know our children—their strengths and weaknesses, their likes and dislikes, their learning style and attention span. What motivates them? What are they interested in or curious about? Identifying your children's interests will make a big difference in the way you introduce family history to them and in the way they respond. Remember, their hobbies and interests can change from year to year as they mature and are exposed to new ideas and people.

Many children want to know more about their family history. I was touched to learn from one woman that her grandson had requested a birthday cake in the shape of a family tree. Not only did she gladly honor his request, she photocopied pictures of her grandson along with his parents and grandparents and arranged them on his family tree cake.

Children need the stability that a knowledge of their roots can give them. A connection to the past can provide a sanctuary for children, says Marcia Smith, Ph.D., psychologist and behavioral science coordinator with Brown University's Family Medicine Residency Program. "Children's roots are part of their identity formation," she notes. "Having something to identify with is extremely important for children. One's family history is a source of pride and self-esteem, even at a very young age."

Yes, it is a challenge to find time in your children's busy schedules of schoolwork, sports, dance and piano lessons, friends, even part-time jobs. Children and teens certainly don't lack for things to do. But sharing time together needn't take more than a few hours a week. The activities in this book are designed to catch their attention and to be fun and interesting. As a parent or grandparent, you are in the best position to adapt the activities toward your children's individual interests.

This book offers numerous ideas and suggestions to help you capture the imagination of your children and focus it on their family tree. Nevertheless, you will need to exercise creativity, ingenuity, and patience. You'll also find a broad array of activities here that are designed to get your own creativity working. Remember that the ideas presented here should act as a springboard; they can and should be modified to fit your individual situation. They may even give you ideas to help you further your own research at the same time. Most importantly, they should help you and your family learn to appreciate your ancestors and each other, and have a lot of fun in the process.

Chapter One

Treasures in the Attic

Children respond to items they can see and touch: a rhinestone brooch from the 1950s, an old report card, a passport, a fragile Christmas tree ornament, a photograph of their grandmother. Although our ancestors are no longer with us, their old photographs, dresses, report cards, jewelry, and knickknacks—these forgotten family treasures in attics, closets, and cellars—can provide a doorway into the past to pique the interest of a potential junior genealogist.

Most families have photographs of Mom and Dad when they were younger, maybe even a wedding picture of Grandma and Grandpa. You might even find older pictures of immigrant ancestors when you begin to search. Old school books with a name written inside in a child's handwriting and especially old toys can have the power to turn your apathetic preteen into a wide-eyed family historian.

Who knows what other articles might have outlived their owners and survived to surprise their descendants? Searching your attic might give you the answer.

Old Photographs

Old photographs offer one of the easiest and most accessible ways to involve your children in their family history. Whether it's a picture of your grandmother's Cousin Netta holding the reins of her horse on a cobblestone street in Scotland or your uncle with the largest watermelon of a good growing season, photographs can play a significant role in sparking interest in genealogy. A picture of your grandfather in his victory garden may prompt your child to ask, "What's a victory garden?"

A photograph is often the most intimate contact your children can have with their ancestors. A family resemblance to a great-great-grandmother or grandfather can lead to a child's interest in that particular ancestor's life, which may lead to questions about that ancestor's parents, siblings, aunts, and uncles. A child looking at a photograph showing four generations of the family may see those similarities in features or stature. He or she might even ask about less obvious similarities or differences. Your granddaughter might be fascinated to discover that the unusual cameo brooch she spots in an old photo of your great-aunt is lying in your old jewelry box. It may even be that you haven't recognized it yourself. A child's keen eyes are often the clue to unlocking secrets from the past.

Photographs can offer great clues to present-day historical mysteries. If your grandfather never spoke about his early years, an old photo may show that he had athletic interests at one time. An old picture of your great-grandfather as a teenager posing in uniform with a field hockey stick just might make your teen want to know more about his great-grandfather and create an interest in his family. Or grandmother at age eight, standing at an outdoor skating rink in February, her hair in pigtails. Beneath the photo is the written caption "Just learning!" While this photo is proof that she had a very different life in the decades before her grandchildren knew her, it may also indicate a life with interests similar to those of her grandchildren who also love outdoor winter sports.

Although photography was still relatively new to many of our more recent ancestors, they did hire photographers for special occasions, so we do have some visual records of them (thank goodness!). Weddings, graduations, and confirmations are all significant occasions, and sometimes, if we are lucky, our ancestors recorded them through photographs. Photos taken at casual outings, such as church picnics or on fishing trips, will allow your children to see a less formal side of their predecessors.

Familiarize yourself with a good book on historic costumes and have it handy for looking at old photos with your children. Make note of details such as collars, sleeves, and waistlines. Look for jewelry such as necklaces or rings that you know belonged to a certain ancestor. Watch for photographer's imprints that can help date the photo. Take your child with you when you look through city directories to find out when a studio was in business or where it was located. Pay particular attention to clues in the backgrounds of photos, such as shops or numbers on houses, that can positively identify the location or the year a picture was taken.

Find pictures of yourself when you were a small child. Identify the other people in the photographs and share the stories of those relationships with your children.

It also helps to have descriptions of your relatives for identification purposes. Knowing whether an ancestor had light or dark hair or whether he was short or tall, heavy or slim enables you to recognize people more easily. Soldiers from the Civil War to the present have traditionally been photographed in uniform. Their uniforms can designate rank or reveal location, helping you pinpoint the date. These portraits also reflect the seriousness of their mission, and the fears and concerns that weighed on their minds.

Group portraits make it easy to differentiate one family member from another. When you know that your great-grandfather had two sisters and three brothers, it becomes less difficult to identify the individuals in a family portrait.

Do some basic research before you try to identify snapshots. Your knowledge of your family history may be enough to identify subjects in photos. If you can, show your children pictures of their ancestors at different ages, especially people they know well, like their grandparents.

"Seeing pictures of people at different ages fascinates children and gives them a feeling of continuity," says Claire Brisson-Banks, director of the Family History Center Library of The Church of Jesus Christ of Latter-day Saints in Warwick, Rhode Island. She adds that if you don't know the subject of a photo, you should admit your lack of knowledge to your children rather than attempt to hide it. They need to know that it's all right not to have all the answers. Perhaps the unknown identity is a mystery you can solve together over time.

Show your children pictures of old automobiles, clothing, and other items that are representative of your ancestors' days.

There are many different angles to catch your children's interest in discussing their immigrant ancestors—the country of origin, the alternatives if they hadn't emigrated, the stories that might have been handed down. At times, immigrants arranged for portraits to be taken before sailing from foreign ports to the wharves of America's waterfront. If you don't have access to such a photo, you can order a photograph of the ship in which your forebears sailed to America from Ellis Island. Those whose ancestors arrived in New York Harbor between 1892 and 1954 can find information electronically from the Immigration Center at Ellis Island, now a national park. Its website is <www.ellisisland.org>. Reproductions of ships' manifests are also available for a fee. Thanks to the federal law that required passenger lists to be kept after 1819, you can probably find the ship on which your ancestors sailed.

"Old photographs are the entryway to information and knowledge," says Ruth Thomasian, executive director of Project SAVE Armenian Photograph Archives. "Everyone responds to visual stimuli. When you look at family pictures you can't help but wonder and want to know more about the people in them."

The only ethnic photograph archives in the United States, Project SAVE aims to preserve all aspects of Armenian life. Ruth shows how various elements of photographs can provide clues to family historians. Details such as a cameo on a dress, a hat style, trees in a landscape, or hair color and complexion can be helpful in identifying photographs that would otherwise remain anonymous. Historic details and styles of dress can help date photos to within a few years. Accessories and backgrounds in photographs can provide clues about the origins of the picture.

Family photographs add warmth to a house and reinforce a child's heritage, identity, and sense of belonging. The hallway of the Loberti family's house features an antique sideboard lined with sepia-toned family portraits. The old photos invite questions from their seven-year-old daughter who sees pictures of people she knows but doesn't recognize. Since children are naturally curious, surrounding them with family photographs is bound to intrigue them. Photos invite curiosity and encourage questions.

Audrey Loberti is currently in the process of organizing modern photographs that have accumulated over the years. "They've been in boxes under the bed for too long," she laments. "But I'm glad I waited. I'll organize them differently now than I would have if I'd put them away at the time." Audrey plans to organize pictures by holidays, beginning with Christmas and birthdays. Now that her daughter is old enough, an ideal way to interest her in her family history is to involve her in the sorting project.

Organizing photographs by themes is a unique way to display treasured pictures and a quick way to revive forgotten memories. The wisest option is to have copies made for display so the originals can be left in albums or in acid-free sleeves where they will be safe from the harmful effects of exposure.

Give your children a stack of unorganized family photographs to delve into and discover. Under your supervision, have them write the names of the subjects in the photo on note cards to be placed behind the picture. Older children could also place the photos in photo albums.

If you don't have a large collection of photographs and you'd like to showcase more photos in your home, ask other family members and relatives for permission to explore their collections. You might be surprised what still exists and how much you can learn from it. You may be able to borrow the originals or pay to have copies made. Having negatives is not as critical as it once was, and digital copiers leave no excuse for not making extra prints.

Once you've assembled your collection of photographs, select a few of the most meaningful ones and display copies. Keep them handy so your children have a constant reminder of their heritage.

Treasures in Hiding

When possible, invite your children to help you sort and discard items from the past as you help clean out the attic or basement of an elderly or recently deceased family member. For many children the tangible articles of the past may be the key to tapping into their curiosity. An aunt's porcelain figurines, an uncle's key chains from around the world, or a grandmother's music boxes can be exciting finds, especially for a older children who already have their own collection of similar objects. And the value of what is found might be less financial than it is personal; their value often rests in helping us learn about our ancestors' lives.

Or you may be lucky enough to have an attic containing assorted objects that belonged to your grandmother or your great-aunt. If these things aren't of great value, let your children examine any old items you have inherited. Articles such as old-fashioned hats, costume jewelry, dishes, handkerchiefs, and knickknacks are fascinating to a young child who hasn't seen them before. Let your child play detective through the process of discovering new things that give them a sense of who their deceased relatives were.

From an old banjo to a silver filigree napkin ring, every object can open a window to the past. These are the kinds of things you can call upon to stimulate your children's interest in genealogy. Ordinary items like button hooks, butter churns, and other articles that are no longer in use today may also catch their interest. Consider the dolls of your own childhood. If they're still in your attic and they aren't extremely rare and valuable collectibles by now, perhaps your eight- or ten-year-old could be entrusted with such a gift.

Photographs and other artifacts of the past are as interesting to older children as they are to younger children. When objects such as these reflect similar interests, they can serve to bridge generations. If any of your children share interests in common with an ancestor, you might encourage him or her to start a collection based on your ancestors' belongings. For example, if you've inherited a great-aunt's collection of china teacups or salt and pepper shakers, or a great-uncle's train set, let it serve as the basis for a collection for one of your children.

In uncovering her ancestor's possessions, one woman discovered salt and pepper shakers, teacups, record albums, and books by the hundreds. The books and records didn't survive years in a musty cellar very well; however, the other items were carefully wrapped and just needed a good cleaning. Among her family's assorted belongings, this woman also found what has amounted to a collection of old Bibles. She has one for each of five generations with family names written inside. Such a treasure could fascinate a child.

Even something as mundane as a collection of records, stamps, spoons, rocks, baseball cards, or hats gives some insight into their owners. Travelers may collect harlequin dolls or African masks, postcards, or maps. People report collecting everything from figurines to wind chimes. These kinds of objects give children insight into the personalities and interests of family members from previous generations.

Boxes in the attic or cellar may contain old photographs, letters, lace gloves, jewelry, or even papers that can prove you're descended from a Revolutionary or Civil War soldier. You may also come across scrapbooks detailing an individual's interests or family events; club, lodge, or fraternal organization memorabilia; or a shoebox full of newspaper clippings related to family activities.

Some families may choose to keep report cards from grammar school or term papers from high school. When her interest in genealogy piqued at the age of fourteen, Kristi Brown received numerous personal effects of her ancestors from relatives, including a report card from 1916. Report cards play such a significant role in the lives of teens, it's hard to imagine that young people today wouldn't be at least a little interested in seeing an ancestor's report card. Kristi also received an old chauffeur's driver's license, which would likewise be of interest since most teens are looking forward to getting their own driver's licenses and are at an age at which their ancestors' occupations are beginning to interest them.

One of my most intriguing discoveries was a hope chest that belonged to my grandmother. Inside was an eclectic collection of objects that included an unopened present. Unwrapping the gift was like giving myself a gift from the past: a brand new pair of bath towels that had never reached its intended recipient.

In addition, the trunk contained various odds and ends that had belonged to several generations of women in our family. The bottom of the trunk was lined with embroidered pieces my great-great-aunts and great-grandmother had stitched: doilies, bureau scarves, tablecloths, lace table runners, hand towels, handkerchiefs—in short, every manner of dainty lace work.

Frame a crocheted doily or embroidered piece by a relative or ancestor to use as an accent for a room. If sewing is your child's hobby, this might make an excellent project.

Also in the trunk were two dozen cotton squares obviously intended to be made into a quilt, all with red stitching on a white background. Each square featured a different picture in a style typical of the late Victorian age—a rooster, a cat, a blossom. Two squares contained information of significance. One square had been stitched with the letter "B" while another was stitched with the year "1892." My great-grandmother Bertha had turned fifteen years old in 1892. The quilt project was obviously unfinished but showed Bertha's early attempts at needlework, making the squares a legacy to treasure. They offer a sewing project that could span generations if I choose to take on the challenge. It's fascinating to find unfinished projects our ancestors started and to try to finish them as we think they might have intended. Such an endeavor is one way to pay homage to our female ancestors.

Perhaps your daughter might be inspired to create her own project after seeing the needlework projects done by her grandmother or great-grandmother. Many young girls learn to use a sewing machine in home economics class and may be interested in sewing projects for school assignments or for their own pleasure. They might enjoy hearing your stories about your own early sewing attempts as well.

When your daughter is old enough to take proper care of the drawstring bag her grandmother crocheted, you might permit her to use it for a special occasion. It will be different from anything anyone else has, and it will be special to her because of its unique history.

As you uncover these treasures you may find your own memories awakened. After telling your children what you remember, take the time to make a written record for yourself and others in your family.

If you have a trunk in the attic with clothing that belonged to your ancestors, let your children play dress up. The differences in style are sure to bring up questions about the people who wore the clothing.

Family Heirlooms

Each family has its own special treasures that are significant to its history. Mary Alice Andrews took the white dress she wore at her wedding in 1891 to Edmund Joseph Anyon and turned it into a christening gown for her son four years later. The act created a familial bond and a family tradition she could never have imagined. The christening gown, which has been handled with meticulous care ever since, was recently worn by another young descendant, Madison McKeen Flaxington. Madison was the forty-seventh child to be christened in the gown.

Made of cotton eyelet, the christening gown is accompanied by a slip and is washed gently by hand between wearings. In recent years, a matching jacket was added to disguise wear in the top of the gown and sleeve openings were enlarged to accommodate today's bigger babies. Ruth Flaxington, Madison's grandmother, cares for the gown and keeps a list of the scores of babies who have worn it and the dates on which they were christened. The list is stored with the gown.

It is important to keep a record of the history of heirlooms as well as a note about their future. Securing their fate in writing helps them to reach their intended recipients. Family historian Barbara Freshwater has discussed her family heirlooms with her daughter, who is the executor of Barbara's estate.

"I've marked the family heirlooms for my daughter," she says. "I've painted portraits of all my female ancestors on plates with their vital statistics baked into the back of the plate. They go as far back as my great-great-grandmothers."

Such heirlooms are meaningful because of their history. Not only is a gift from the past being passed on to a new generation, but there is the sense that it carries the blessings of its original owner when it goes to a direct descendant.

Anna Haukness says her heirloom is her mother's Hungarian Bible that survived the war camps of Europe during World War II. Anna's mother was raised in Hungary but was originally of Russian and German descent. The daughter of prosperous Russian parents whose fortunes began to decline during the Russian Revolution, she became a war orphan during her childhood as the family moved throughout Europe.

Somehow the family's Bible survived and reached America with the family. "It is especially poignant because it was so difficult to keep anything," Anna says. "The family was at the mercy of the Red Cross and was always moving."

Because of the difficulty of continual travel, always trying to stay several steps ahead of the front line, they lost nearly all of their personal possessions as they traveled across the continent. Having survived the hardships and sacrifices of the war, Anna says, the worn sheepskin Bible has special significance to her mother.

These items need not have great monetary value; in many cases their value comes from you and your attachment to them. Audrey Loberti counts her grandmother's pepper biscuit pot among her treasures. While Audrey was growing up her mother's mother always kept her pepper biscuits, an Italian staple, in a bulky porcelain pitcher. Once used to pour coffee or tea, the vessel is now speckled with cracks and hasn't been used in years for its intended purpose. Audrey remembers her grandmother making pepper biscuits, wrapping them in plastic, and putting them in the pot, inviting family members to help themselves.

Nor does an item need a long history to make it an heirloom. Anna Lindsey's grandmother's picnic basket, complete with tablecloth, dishes, and utensils, was a wonderful discovery after her father's death, especially since his mother had died over fifty years before. Anna had seen the picnic basket in photographs and knew it was well traveled throughout the Northeast. She could even document where it had been based on photographs.

Consider Aunt Etta's iced tea pitcher and matching glasses along with your grandmother's large red glass bowl or the tiny matching dishes for old-fashioned grapenut pudding (a favorite in our family). These treasures may be delicate, but if you haven't used them in years you might as well start now. Put them out for Sunday dinner or for a Saturday afternoon chat with your daughter. Doing so will help you share memories with your children and grandchildren that may last a lifetime.

Perhaps your grandfather or great-grandfather tried his hand at carving a weather vane or other wooden object at one time. If so, you may find something he made tucked away somewhere. Many women produced colorful quilts and a variety of embroidered pieces. Such handmade items might have been saved for sentimental reasons and stored away along with old furniture. What a treasure any one of these items would be for a child.

Take a few minutes and picture your house as you were growing up. Think of the objects you remember most fondly. Perhaps they are articles that represent a certain individual of whom you are reminded every time you see them. I remember playing with a black cocker spaniel figurine, inexpensive but beloved, that now occupies a special place in my curio cabinet. The day will come when my daughters will be third-generation owners. When it is passed on, I want them to appreciate its history even though they never knew the grandmother from whom it came.

Creating a tabletop display of your favorite historical items with photographs, a baby's silver spoon, a pretty floral teacup with sentimental value, dried bouquets or flowers, lace embroidery, candlesticks, or a delicate antique vase.

As you let your children explore the cellar, encourage them to tap the memories of their living relatives regarding specific items they find. The women in the family are more likely to remember details about a fruit bowl on a dining room table than are the men in the family, while the men may be better able to discuss the kinds of automobiles driven by the family in the past and what tools were used.

While many family heirlooms have been set aside for posterity, some have yet to be discovered. Attics and cellars are repositories for treasures that remain hidden for years, or are often forgotten. They come to light after the death of a relative or after someone cleans out and decides to pass them on, when the objects are reincarnated and appreciated once again. Take a good look at these hiding places with your children and see what comes to light.

Make a family quilt for your children using old pieces of fabric, quilt squares you find, or snippets from old clothing, kitchen towels, and other household fabrics (nothing is quite as personal as the clothing someone has worn). Ask everyone in the family for a fabric swatch from an old item of clothing that's going to be thrown out soon. If you find a quilt is too ambitious, try a pillow. You might even give all the family members a pair of scissors and get them involved.

Heirloom Jewelry

People often save and preserve jewelry not just for the monetary value it may have, but because the pieces are associated with the individuals who wore them. In many cases, a family story is behind a loved one's piece of jewelry. The combination of the two is often an irresistible one for children.

Because jewelry is often distinct and recognizable, it is a clue that can help you and your children identify photographs. If an elderly relative happens to recognize an old photo of a woman wearing a black ring you've seen in your mother's collection, you now know to whom the onyx originally belonged. Likewise, if someone recognizes a brooch as belonging to Great-Grandma Frances, and you find a photo from the 1870s of a woman wearing the same brooch, chances are good that you've identified the subject. What an exciting discovery for your child to make with you.

After my mother passed away, I found among her belongings a neatly folded piece of tissue in which lay an exquisitely delicate ring. The intricate carvings on the tiny band were set with three opals that sparkled in pastel shades. As I studied the ring I realized it was too old to have originated with my mother. Then I remembered my great-aunt telling me that my great-great-grandfather had given each of his daughters a birthstone ring. Here, I realized with excitement, was the opal that had belonged to Aunt Min, the only one of the five with an October birthday.

Aunt Min had left the ring to her niece, my father's mother. My grandmother in turn had given it to her new daughter-in-law, whose birthday was the same month as Aunt Min's, since it is considered bad luck for anyone not born in October to wear opals. The ring seemed destined for my mother.

Also meaningful are fraternal emblems or pieces of jewelry that represent an organization with which your ancestor was affiliated. Finding such pieces of jewelry reveals the interests and values of the owner, which in turn can help your children or grandchildren see their ancestors as real people.

Years back when Beverly Winger was installed as worthy advisor of her local Rainbow chapter, she wore the ring her mother had worn thirty years earlier when she was a Rainbow Girl. "It meant a great deal to me to have my mother's ring," she says. "It was more special than anything new that I could have bought. I plan to pass it on to my daughter when her turn comes."

Chapter Two

Activities You Can Do at Home

Depending on the ages of your children, encouraging their interest in family history can involve a bit of strategy. Nevertheless, you will find many simple things you can do at home that require little or no special preparation. You may have already experienced some degree of success by using photographs to introduce your children to their ancestors. Continue to build on your early successes by telling the stories behind the family photos and other heirlooms you may have in your possession. Tell your children about the cedar chest Grandpa made for Grandma when they were married. People have always been captivated by stories, and you will find that your children are no exception. If you're not comfortable with your own storytelling abilities just yet, you might simply share a favorite book from your own childhood. It may well lead into stories from your own early days or memories of your parents, siblings, friends, or school days.

In addition to telling stories, you will find several family games to help jumpstart memories and communication. Some computer games on the market also simulate living in the past so families can experience life as their ancestors did. You can also make up games to introduce your ancestors to your family. On the eve of a holiday of historical significance, such as Independence Day or Thanksgiving, sit down with your children and discuss the holiday and its importance to your ancestors. You'll be amazed at the many things you'll find to do once you get started.

Family Stories

Generally speaking, bedtime is the best opportunity to tell family stories since children are winding down and tend to be more inclined to listen. Share with them your own adventures as a child or those of your parents and grandparents. Tell a children's story about someone from your family history. (Or experiment until you find a favorite story, perhaps one from history, that your child will enjoy.)

"Parents often get tired of telling the same old bedtime stories to their children," says David Lambert, library manager of the New England Historic Genealogical Society. "Tell family stories instead. Tell about your life or their grandparents' lives." David believes that the physical trappings of genealogy—photographs, letters, and even gravestones—are useful but ultimately impermanent. It is stories, he feels, that will keep children interested into old age.

One family's favorite story relates how their grandfather handled the housekeeping during his wife's absence. Rather than wash the dinner dishes he turned them over and used them again. This incident has been greatly enjoyed by the grandchildren, who watched as they sat at the table, and has given them an endearing memory of their grandfather.

How about the story of Aunt Ida's little dog who followed her everywhere and died within days of her beloved owner's death? Or the summer the children all had whooping cough and Mother dragged the mattresses out into the front yard so the children could sleep outside where it was cool? Once you start telling stories, you'll find that they seem to keep coming.

But don't limit yourself to these few minutes at bedtime. A parent who is running errands with children in the car may have a captive audience for stories of long ago. Vacations are also good opportunities to share family stories, and they can make a long drive go much more quickly. Your children may not enjoy the same stories or feel drawn to the same ancestors as you, but you'll learn over time what stories they enjoy hearing again and again. Mix some humorous stories with the more serious and dramatic stories of your ancestors.

If you don't have any colorful stories to tell, do some more research. Look for stories of people who lived in the same place and time that your ancestors did. If you have an ancestor who was a farmer in Oklahoma during the Depression, read about the people and their experiences. Although your ancestor may not have kept a diary, other people who lived in the same region and experienced the same challenges of weather and sickness may have kept one. On a ship of several hundred immigrants to a new country, one or two individuals may have kept a written record that is now a part of a library's special collections or in the archives of a state historical society. Those records will help you gain perspective of your own ancestors' lives, and will give you more stories to share with your children.

Your children's interest in genealogy doesn't have to stem from your own family. You can inspire your children with someone else's story. In a book of reminiscences by Civil War veterans, one man said that the most memorable event of his service was shaking hands with President Lincoln at City Point, Virginia, in 1865. In the same book, I learned that my great-great-grandfather felt the most important part of his service in the Civil War was "our march from Burksville Station to Danville to cut off Johnson's retreat. We marched a hundred twelve miles in five days." The first story meant much more to my six-year-old daughter, who knew of Abraham Lincoln but had never heard of Burksville.

Your ancestors needn't be famous to be the subject of colorful stories. What about the time your great-grandfather was working as a boy and got locked in the neighborhood grocery store overnight? Maybe your great-great-great-great-grandfather the clockmaker was asked to design a clock for George Washington. Share with your children the accomplishments and details of your ancestors' lives. Those are the stories that will make them come to life in your children's eyes.

Family Night

Schedule an evening, or perhaps set aside Sunday afternoon, to spend time with your family. Look at family photographs, play a game, or watch one of the historical videos suggested later in this book. When two different families were asked how they managed to keep their families close, each described their tradition of observing a "Family Night."

The Salloways have observed the custom of their Friday Shabbat ritual for twenty-five years, since before their two children were born. Kim Salloway says she can count on one hand the number of Fridays her husband has missed it due to conflicts. He has always arranged to have Friday night off even if it meant working part of the weekend.

"No matter how harried the week is, no matter how divergent our interests and commitments, we always know we have that time when we can be together as a family," says Kim Salloway. That persistence has allowed their Family Night to take hold and grow over the years as a tradition.

The evening consists of candles and a special meal in keeping with Jewish tradition. Each family member reflects on the week that has just ended as well as any particular challenges and plans for the week ahead. The family shares a home-centered activity such as working on a photograph album, playing cards or a board game, or watching a movie.

"It's our way of establishing parameters around the hectic events of the week," Kim says, adding that the family also "works on ways to find closure to issues that might not have gone as well as we would have liked. Family issues are addressed as well as outside concerns. We reflect on things we're grateful for as a family. In doing so we celebrate a variety of blessings."

With Family Night a lifelong tradition, her sixteen-year-old son and fourteen-year-old daughter respect the customs upheld by their parents. When the teenagers began to have conflicting interests that threatened to interfere with the Friday routine, the parents compromised by allowing them to invite friends for dinner and evening activities. That decision has allowed their children to share their religion while giving friends a chance to learn about Judaism.

While it requires persistence and commitment for most families to adhere faithfully to such a routine, the results are worth it. This tradition has enriched the Salloways' lives by allowing them to build a close-knit family that can grow together in an atmosphere of mutual trust, compassion, and love. Each Friday night provides an example of teamwork and togetherness as it contributes to a lifetime of memories of shared joys and concerns.

"I could never put a price on the time we spend together," Kim notes. "Every Friday night we're creating memories the family will have for a lifetime."

The Brickels are another family who observes a family night; however, their family night falls on Mondays. The evening begins with a song and prayer, followed by a poem or scripture reading. Family members take turns each week giving the prayer, reading a scripture, leading the lesson, and preparing refreshments. All children who are old enough take turns teaching a lesson, often with the assistance of one of the parents. Lessons may involve hand-drawn or colored visual aids, or a game designed to teach principles and practices.

Families may hold home evenings by performing other family activities as well. Family games, picnics, service projects, hiking, cultural events, gardening, vacation planning, or recreational activities are also suitable activities for their home evening. The focus is on activities that bring the family together.

Regardless of how you choose to spend your time as a family, begin by establishing and maintaining a "Family Night" in your household. Allow no distractions or exceptions. Prepare a favorite meal together, and then watch a historical movie about the country of your immigrant ancestors. Plan a family vacation together or microwave some popcorn and pull out some family videos or an old photograph album. Let your children see what life was like when you were young. They'll undoubtedly laugh at the clothing and hairstyles of your day.

Games and Activities

Depending on the ages of your children, you can have a lot of fun with games of imagination and adventure. When my daughter was four, she loved to play "pirates." We would construct a pirate ship out of boxes, duct tape, and black construction paper. Then we would add paper masts and a flag along with two wheels to use to steer her by (one for each of us). Cardboard tubes served as telescopes, and paper hats with big feathers completed our accessories. You may want to play this game and relate it to an immigrant ancestor or sailor in your family, and discuss your destination and food stores with your child.

> **Buy a globe of the world and show your children the countries your ancestors came from. It's a good introduction to the family's background, and a great geography lesson.**

Young children may also enjoy making whimsical paper dolls that represent their ancestors. This is a great project for children and easy if you're handy with scissors. For the faces, photocopy pictures of your ancestors or use modern family pictures as substitutes. (If all else fails, cut faces from magazines.) Draw and cut out the bodies on cardboard or trace them from other paper dolls. Consult a library book on historic costumes for clothing designs. You can either color the costumes or glue fabric to thin cardboard cutouts. You can also buy some wonderful and inexpensive historic paper dolls (Victorian, Pilgrim, and dolls from various ethnic backgrounds) if you don't feel overly creative or don't have the time to make them.

Another time one of my daughters and I created a diorama with a set of plastic jungle animals and then built a habitat for them. We glued sticks and strips of green tissue paper for the trees, then glued white paper clouds onto a blue sky, and rocks and sand along the bottom of the box to form the terrain. A similar project would be to make small paper figures to place on board a ship, in a castle, in a log cabin, or in a nineteenth-century tenement house. Each of these activities provide an opportunity to teach your child about the lives of your ancestors.

Games specifically oriented to the family are especially appropriate, and although they may take a little preparation, the family response may well be worth it. A set of Bingo cards made with the faces from family photographs can make the game more interesting, especially if the faces are from little-known ancestors. Match games can be made to match faces of ancestors with biographical information. Or, for immigrant ancestors you may even try to "pin the ship on the port" or the "covered wagon on the plain" and use a map to mark the trail.

A popular game for families is *LifeStories*®, a Parents' Choice Award Winner, by the makers of the popular *Ungame*®, another excellent communications game. *LifeStories* is described as a jumpstart for family storytelling and a noncompetitive game designed to get the family talking and asking questions. Another family game, the *Family Tree Trivia Game*, is available at <www.heartscorner.com>.

Computer games with an historic focus is another way you can entice your child to explore the world of the past. You will find a growing number of these on the market, with more appearing all the time. One of my daughter's favorite games is *Oregon Trail*, which allows children to be pioneers as they encounter hazards on their journey from Missouri to Oregon. The game simulates the hardships faced by our pioneer ancestors including flooded rivers, broken wagon wheels, difficult mountain passes, disease, and rough weather. Players purchase supplies for the journey at various trading posts and must rely on their hunting skills to keep from starving. The game challenges children by increasing their knowledge of map-reading skills, westward expansion, and geography.

For older children who enjoy games of strategy, introduce them to the Avalon Hill series. With *Battle Cry*, players command Union and Confederate armies in authentic battles, determining how many regiments to send into combat and other strategies. As a tool for teaching about World War II, *Axis and Allies* also has many fans. These types of games are fun as well as educational and put history at children's fingertips.

On a map of the United States, place a sticker on each town or county where your ancestors used to live. Trace the path of their migration from town to town.

Holidays and Civic Events

Many holidays are celebrated at the city and community level and can provide opportunities to teach children about their ancestors. For example, Thanksgiving and Memorial Day parades give families an enjoyable way to recognize the historical contributions of others. Celebrating history with other people can often be more inspiring than trying to do it on your own.

"For us, Memorial Day includes a huge parade in the village where I was born," says Lisa Mather. "My grandfather is a World War II vet and is always at the front of the parade. My daughter enjoys this and we always try to wear something red, white, and blue!"

While many holidays are celebrated throughout the United States and Canada, some are particular to city, state, or region. For example, Massachusetts celebrates Patriots Day every April by reenacting the battles of Lexington and Concord, which opened the American Revolution. Rhode Island's Gaspee Days celebration each spring commemorates the burning of the English ship, *The Gaspee,* during the Revolutionary War. Similarly, Utah celebrates Pioneer Day on July 24th, the day pioneers entered the Salt Lake Valley in 1847, with parades, fireworks, costumes, and other festivities, and Canada celebrates Victoria Day, which provides an opportunity for families to talk about history and immigrant ancestors. If your community has a similar celebration, take the time to discuss its significance with your children when the holiday approaches.

Celebrate Independence Day or another historic holiday with authentic food and costumes from the past, and discuss the events with your children.

If your ancestors were among the early pioneers who explored the American West, build a cabin out of Lincoln Logs™. Make clothespin dolls to inhabit your home and sew or glue cotton outfits for them. Tell stories about your pioneer ancestors; if you have little record of their lives, look at the records other pioneers have left for information on their travels, hardships, recreation, and other aspects of their lives.

You could also celebrate another ancestor's birthday as a way to teach your children about that ancestor's life. Wrap a few mementos that belonged to that person as "presents" and let your children take turns opening them, then tell the story behind each of the objects. The refreshments you serve at the party might even be the favorite treat of the ancestor (if you know what it was and have a recipe).

Some cities host special festivities that are not associated with holidays or particular events. Rather, the purpose is to inform local people and visitors about the town and area. Worcester, Massachusetts, sponsors an annual "street sampler," a tour of buildings and sites of importance to the city and its history. People are invited to visit churches, libraries, and museums, and view special exhibits, demonstrations, and other historical attractions.

Activities like these may be sponsored by historical and heritage societies, city tourism boards, and ethnic heritage and preservation commissions. Watch for announcements of other parades and heritage celebrations being held in your area. They may be city- or state-sponsored, and they offer a fun way to introduce your children to your town's or state's roots as well as the heritage of its early inhabitants.

Depending on where you live, you will find a variety of activities suitable for families with children. Many times you will find activities particularly geared to children. Rhode Island's state historical society runs a series of week-long history camps with morning or afternoon sessions for children entering grades four through six. The four-hour sessions include historic games, crafts, stories, tours, and related activities. Camps like this offer idyllic summer afternoons spent enjoying the amusements of earlier times.

The Museum of Primitive Art and Culture, also in Rhode Island, sponsors an afternoon of "Games from Grandparents' Childhood." This activity is a perfect excuse to bring your children and your parents as well. These activities are designed specifically for children and target age-appropriate interests, providing an attraction that is fun and educational. It entertains both generations while connecting them. Check publications in your area for activities that relate to your past and seek these activities out. Your children will be glad you did.

Chapter Three

Fun with History

The differences between children of today and yesterday are so vast that it can be difficult for our children to understand what life in the past was like. Consider the boundaries of your child's life at home, at school, and at play, and compare them to those of earlier generations. As you help your children see what life was like in the nineteenth century, they will begin to understand more clearly the differences between their ancestors and themselves.

One advantage we have as family historians is that most of our nineteenth-century immigrant ancestors were average working people. The good news is that not only do we have a great deal in common with our ancestors, but there is also a great deal of documented material available on the lives of ordinary citizens. Most of our ancestors were concerned with putting food on the table for their families, earning enough to pay the rent until they could afford their own home, raising their children to be morally upright and properly behaved, helping to find a husband for the eldest daughter—usually a man of her own nationality—and often setting aside enough money to bring other family members to America from their native homeland.

Children are often surprised to learn that in the 1870s their great-great-great-uncle went to work at the mill at the tender age of seven. Since many of our ancestors were forced to leave school and work to help support their families, a diploma from grammar school or junior high was an item of exceptional worth well into the first four decades of the 1900s. Many people did not continue school beyond the age of fourteen, and some ended their formal schooling earlier than that.

Teenagers in high school are especially receptive to learning about their ancestors' occupations, says Claire Brisson-Banks, especially if the type of work is something that has been handed down over generations. Claire has conducted numerous family history projects with teenagers in high school, and has been the director of the local LDS Family History Center in Warwick, Rhode Island, since 1988.

Recreate a tea party from your great-aunt's day. This will give your children a chance to dress up and enjoy ice cream sundaes and croquet (or other suitable refreshment and activity).

"Children often have a new respect for their family once they've learned the kinds of things their ancestors did," she says. "They have a deeper interest in the past than we realize. They have a sense of pride in their ancestors' accomplishments."

Life in the Past

If you were to ask your children what activities make up their lives today, they would probably mention school, baseball games or piano lessons, family activities, vacations, birthdays, computer games, and movies. If you were to ask what they expected for the future, they might mention college, careers, travel, and families.

Now compare this to what expectations may have been for young people in earlier times. A book from the library might show pictures of children working in mills and describe the long hours they were forced to work. At times children were so exhausted that they fell asleep on the job, which often led to injuries. In the 1800s, only one in four children lived past the age of sixteen; a third of deaths each year were to children under the age of five. Statistics such as these, as well as infant mortality rates will help your children understand the advances of modern medicine.

Have your children list daily activities, chores, school, leisure time choices, vacations, and shopping trips, then make a chart comparing a modern child's life with that of a nineteenth-century child's life. A second chart could compare life expectancies for children living in the nineteenth and twentieth centuries.

When a building is torn town, talk with your children about why things change and how similar changes may have impacted their ancestors' lives.

Your children might be surprised to learn that a century ago most families lived geographically closer to one another than they do today—which was both a comfort and an economic necessity in many cases. Families in close proximity to each other did not have the difficulties of families separated by great distances, but even so they often found ingenious ways to communicate before telephones became popular. For example, my Great-Great-Aunt Nan used to hang a towel out the window when she wanted something from the store. It was a signal to her niece Mae, who could see Nan's pantry window from her own home a block away.

Make the most of every story that might fascinate your child. It doesn't matter if you don't know everything about your ancestors. Fill in the blanks with what you know from history. Why did your ancestors decide to leave Ireland in the 1850s? What happened to the family? In many instances, the simplest, most ordinary story may be one that will captivate children the most. One woman loved to hear her mother tell how she put on plays in her backyard and charged safety pins for admission.

It may be helpful to give your school-age children a bit of historical background when you introduce them to ancestors they've never heard of. Tell them who was president and what events were taking place in the United States during your ancestors' lives. Even children today might appreciate that the highlight of a great-great-grandfather's life was listening to President Lincoln's speech in Virginia as the Civil War came to a close.

Even if your children don't rush off to the library to learn more, these initial activities will plant a seed of interest. Whatever their day-to-day activities are, your children may find themselves comparing their lives to those of their ancestors. The differences will amaze them.

School History and Genealogy Projects

Many family historians cite school projects as having been essential in raising their awareness of their ancestors. Juliana Smith, editor of the *Ancestry Daily News,* suggests that one of the best times to focus on family history is while working on history homework with your children.

When children begin a study of their ancestors, it helps them to have some knowledge of the period in question to have an understanding of what it was like to live in a different time. What an eye-opening moment for your eight-year-old to realize that those who shared her last name 150 years ago did not have electricity, cars, television, or indoor plumbing—and even more shocking to realize that some children her own age were already in the workforce. If you have been sharing stories with your children, they may already have some understanding of what their ancestors' lives were like. A school project on the westward expansion, the Gold Rush, the railroad, the Depression, or another topic may give you even more opportunities to talk with your children about their ancestors and the times in which they lived.

Through their diverse school projects, students in Patti Jordan's fourth-grade class learned about three different individuals—a woman who served as a missionary in China for more than thirty years, a man who was a child in the years before World War II, and one student's 106-year-old great-aunt. One student learned that her aunt had worked as a midwife, delivering more than 300 babies, including three of her own grandchildren.

Historical Books

Even when your children are very young, they can enjoy stories about knights and other heroes. Children have long been intrigued by tales of knights and the medieval age, and they are never too young to have their lives enriched by stories about heroes from history. Telling stories about the past helps to build an interest in days gone by.

Nonfiction historical children's books are also helpful in teaching your child about life in the past. These help create for young children (generally under the age of ten) the mindset of another age by putting history in a context they can relate to. *How Children Lived* by Chris and Melanie Rice (Dorling Kindersley, 1995) is a picture book with brief descriptions of everyday life for children in sixteen time periods ranging from ancient Egypt to Renaissance Italy to 1920s America. Keeping children in touch with their heritage is easier when they have a sense of history and can see how their ancestors fit into the picture.

You can also find books with a historical or cultural focus. A moving Civil War story for older elementary school children is Patricia Polacco's *Pink and Say* (Philomel Books, 1994). There are also many well-written and beautifully illustrated children's books in historical fiction and nonfiction on the market as well as ethnic tales. Older children often enjoy historical fiction by Ann Rinaldi, whose historical novels frequently demonstrate the devastating effects of war as seen through the eyes of young women. Her narrators include a bondswoman to John and Abigail Adams, the daughters of Paul Revere and Patrick Henry, and a young Southern woman during the Civil War.

Historical Movies and Videos

Watching historical movies with your children is an easy way to expose them to history. Films that focus on historical elements from war to social manners not only relay information about the past but also invoke a feel for another time period. History comes to life on video in details such as costumes, carriages, and characters that speak and behave in a very different way than children today do. Children can learn a lot by watching the diverse lifestyles of the poor and the wealthy, seeing the hardships children faced in the past, and learning about the social expectations confronting their ancestors. Films set in the Victorian age illustrate this particularly well, as portrayed in *Pride and Prejudice, David Copperfield,* and many others.

For younger children, most libraries carry Scholastic's "Dear America" series of videos that show a variety of American experiences for both immigrants and colonial children. Check your local library

Visit living history museums and historical sites with costumed interpreters. It's much easier to imagine your ancestors' lives as you walk among ladies in full-length cloaks and bonnets. Such a visit will allow your children to see firsthand how their ancestors lived. Try an old mill, a historic fort, or even a Renaissance fair.

for those and similar types of videos. Movies such as *Sarah, Plain and Tall* and *O Pioneers!* give children a sense of pioneer settlers and immigration, while *White Fang* or *Iron Will* contain glimpses of life in the Yukon. *Little Women* captures family life in Massachusetts with the father away fighting in the Civil War.

Public television for children offers *Liberty's Kids* as a fun learning experience about the Revolutionary War. Young children can often relate to different time periods better when they can put a familiar face to the era. Reruns of *Little House on the Prairie* or *The Waltons* also offer children a picture of life in an earlier day. Disney's musical *Newsies* gives a glimpse of lives of young newspaper carriers in 1899 who decided to strike for more pay.

Find historical sites with a connection to your children's hobbies and interests, such as a train museum for a young boy or historical society exhibit of Victorian clothing and accessories for a teenage girl. Visit different types of museums while you're traveling as well.

For older children, historical films with war themes can stimulate an interest in the past. Unfortunately, many of these are R-rated and viewing them is best left to parents' discretion. I found it an unforgettable experience to see Colonel Robert Gould Shaw in *Glory* leading the 54th Massachusetts, the first black regiment, into the jaws of death at Fort Wagner. I was filled with respect and awe seeing the 20th Maine repel the attacking rebels in the movie *Gettysburg.* In both films, the stark contrast between the blue Federal uniforms and the ragtag gray Confederate uniforms gave a clear sense of the desperate determination felt by both sides. Older war movies are less graphic but still powerful. A classic film on World War I, *All Quiet on the Western Front,* shows the senselessness of war (many viewers prefer the original); among the many

World War II movies, an excellent one is *Hell Is for Heroes.*

Films set in a country associated with a family's genealogical heritage can give children a pictorial view of their ancestors' homeland. (As with the films described above, some of these, such as *Braveheart* and *Rob Roy,* are also R-rated.) These and other films connected with historical places, like *The Joy Luck Club, Far and Away,* and even the fanciful *Princess Cariboo,* can inspire an interest in other countries, their peoples, and histories, and create a desire to know more.

The History Channel also provides a great variety of programs on a wide range of topics from ancient Ireland to World War II, all designed to raise awareness of the trials our ancestors faced and to invite further curiosity.

Invite a costumed reenactor to speak at your child's school or the public library. This is a wonderful way to create interest in historical events that children might otherwise find dull in a classroom setting.

Living Histories and Historical Reenactments

Living histories and historical reenactments offer a glimpse of the past though first-person scenarios and help children see history through the eyes of a role player. The differences lie in the length of time and level of personal involvement required. Generally, a living history is observed whereas a reenactment requires participation.

Living histories are often held on town greens, in historic houses, or in national parks as part of National Park Service tours. The events are typically small and last all day; in contrast, reenactments might take place over a weekend. Both of them feature a firing demonstration performed by Civil War reenactors.

Tim Bingham serves as second corporal and acting color sergeant for the 8th Connecticut. His duties for the Union regiment include wood and water detail and assigning guard duty to the men in his unit. Tim notes that reenacting is not only a great family activity, but that children of various ages can play a role.

"The camping experience gives kids a chance to make new friends while learning about history," he says. "My son spent his first three years at reenactments running about in a grain sack and trying to eat dandelions."

Because of liability issues, most reenactors are not allowed on the battlefield with a weapon until they are sixteen years old or, in some cases, eighteen. The experience gives older boys a chance to familiarize themselves with guns while learning the dangers of using weapons. Since musicians in the Civil War tended to be younger, a typical twelve-year-old today might portray a unit's drummer boy. Playing the fife or drum is a manageable role for children and serves the purpose of maintaining historical accuracy within a regiment. Although there are different dress protocols for children, youngsters are also expected to wear period costumes. A twelve-year-old girl would perform the activities of an adult woman, such as cooking or mending.

Civil War reenactments offer spectators a chance to see firsthand many aspects of military life of those who fought in the war. For example, a stroll through the line of tents, or the company street, shows some marked differences between the Confederate and Union military lifestyle. Many Confederate tents are comfortable and elegant, often featuring writing desks, rocking chairs, and Oriental rugs. Union tents are functional and contain only the bare necessities that the men could carry on their backs. Inside a sparsely furnished hospital tent a surgeon wields a bone saw, an instrument most soldiers avoided at all costs.

"At a reenactment you might talk about the Red Sox and the Yankees or the Internet when you're not on the battlefield," Tim says. "At a living history the actor stays in character all the time. I might talk about the rebels up on the hill even if I'm the only one who can see them."

Many groups include some form of educational program in addition to historical preservation. Battery B First Rhode Island Light Artillery, a living history reenactment group dedicated to keeping alive the memory of Civil War veterans, also gives authentic portrayals of historic figures. Their public program includes a tent display with a soldier and equipment, and children are allowed to try on uniforms. The program also includes a display of original medical artifacts and a toy collection that children can play with. The grand finale is a sing-along session around a campfire.

Rent historical videos or watch the History Channel. The programs about historical events might spark your children's interest in the past.

One of the more interesting and fun ways for a family to enjoy history is to become Civil War reenactors. Expectations vary greatly, but regiments usually require that participants dress in authentic period clothing. Not only is reenacting an interesting and unusual way to learn about history, but it also gives children a chance to make friends while they spend a weekend camping with the family.

Reenactments are held throughout the United States and Canada and in Europe as well. With the larger events taking place in Virginia, Pennsylvania, and Maryland, most are held in state parks, farmers' fields, or even cow pastures, while some battles take place on the original battlefield. Reenactors always know the history of the battle they are recreating.

The experience gives children an almost firsthand look at history. Historian Jane Lancaster, Ph.D., notes that reenacting is a valuable experience for encouraging children's interest in their family history. Sometimes the spoken word is not enough to generate a child's interest in history, she says. Watching a reenactment or participating in one can be very helpful.

Participation in civilian reenacting can educate children regarding nineteenth-century society during the Civil War period without the military aspects. It is also a way to help them understand that domestic life continues in times of war. The Sumterville Civilians is a reenactment group that represents life during the Civil War days outside the military. The wives of several reenactors decided to branch out on their own and focus on the social history of the Victorian age and portray the lives of ordinary people.

Some states have their own historic holidays. If your travels bring you near a community celebration, take the time to stop with your family and learn more.

"For so long history was politics and wars," said Heather Wasilewski, one of the Sumterville Civilians. "There was no context for other events that occurred as a part of daily life."

The Sumterville Civilians give presentations at schools, at historic houses, and in other public arenas, demonstrating various aspects of Victorian life. The group also holds children's fairs and educates the public about the lack of sanitation during the Civil War.

You'll also find a variety of reenactors throughout the United States at places such as Living History Farms in Urbandale, Iowa, where historical interpreters perform the daily routines of early Midwestern settlers. At Plimoth Plantation in Massachusetts, you can see Pilgrims going about their daily tasks, and at Old Sturbridge Village, also in Massachusetts, you can watch reenactors as they portray life in a New England village in the 1830s.

If your interests run to other time periods, or if the idea of investing in period costumes, weapons, and ammunition, and participating in regularly scheduled weekend reenactments is too overwhelming a commitment, a Renaissance fair is another great way to inspire your child's imagination. Additionally, the Society for Creative Anachronism gives children and their families a chance to step back into the Middle Ages by assuming a medieval identity (see page 66).

Whatever you choose, encourage your child's active participation in historical events and watch them develop a personal connection to history and related activities.

Reenactment Links

American Revolution
http://americanrevolution.org

War of 1812
www.battleofgeorgianbay.huronia.com

Civil War
www.cwreenactors.com
www.gettysburgreenactment.com

Chapter Four

Family History for Beginners

Parents and grandparents who are still living in the home state of their ancestors will find many places to take their young genealogists-in-training to begin their work. Cemeteries can be great places to introduce budding family historians to the mysteries of genealogy, and churches are often right next door to them. Libraries and LDS Family History Centers are also useful research facilities and they needn't be intimidating, even for young genealogists. Far less likely to intimidate your junior genealogist is the Internet, with its databases, message and bulletin boards, online collections, and more. Now is also the time to introduce your children to older relatives, who can be valuable resources and provide precious information. Family reunions can also be great sources of information, wherever they may be held.

Whether it's copying names and dates off gravestones in cemeteries or photocopying in a library, help your children contribute to their family history by letting them assist you whenever possible. Children need to have a role in order to feel the same fulfillment you feel upon discovering a new ancestor.

Churches and Cemeteries

You may find some surprises not far beyond your own backyard. For three hundred years one branch of my family lived in just three towns on the Rhode Island/Massachusetts border. I discovered the grave of my fifth-great-grandmother in a tiny historic cemetery only a five minute walk from the house in which I grew up. I never learned of its existence until I was an adult, even though I passed the cemetery daily walking home from elementary school.

The cemetery is a good place to visit as long as the children can be supervised while you do your research. Children who are old enough to count can be assigned simple tasks such as counting the number of gravestones from the edge of the road to their great-grandfather's grave.

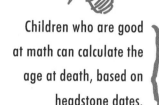

Children who are good at math can calculate the age at death, based on headstone dates.

Sometimes parents of young children have to be inventive to find time to pursue their roots. Visits to local cemeteries may be a surprising way to combine fun and education in identifying "missing" relatives, matching children with parents, and learning the birthplaces of ancestors.

Encouraging your children to take an active interest and play a role in your search is an effective way to ensure their continued interest. One woman includes her children, who range in age from nine to seventeen, on trips to the cemetery and the library, where she gives them surnames to search for and money for the copy machine.

Michael John Neill, a popular lecturer on genealogy topics, encourages parents to have a picnic, letting children create maps of paths to gravestones, and doing some cleanup work around Great-Grandpa's plot. Entrusting your children with such responsibility gives them a real sense that they are contributing something of importance to the family.

"When our kids were little and money was tight," says Lisa Murdough, "we would pack a picnic and go cemetery stomping. Each tyke got a file card with the name Morse printed in big letters, and they would help us look for Morse gravestones. They got some little treat for every one they found. Then we would spell out the words on the stone as I'd copy the info into my notebook. They got a mini spelling lesson, plus some fresh air and sunshine. The research got done, and we all got a bit of exercise and spent the day together."

At the cemetery, young children can search for headstones with their last name. Older children can make maps or copy the writing on the stones.

Sometimes you will find surprises in the cemetery. For many years, a headstone for my great-grandmother was never erected and my mother didn't know why. When she took me to the cemetery, we were surprised to find a stone that read, "MOTHER," and beneath it in smaller letters, "Mother of A. Barnes." (My great-grandmother's name was Elizabeth Barnes.)

We learned from the cemetery office that Uncle Arthur, my great-grandmother's youngest son, had had the stone erected decades after her funeral in 1930. My great-grandmother never wanted a headstone because she had remarried upon coming to America but the marriage had failed. She didn't want "that rotter's name" to be on her tombstone. Seems like Uncle Arthur found a clever way to respect her wishes while revering her memory with a headstone.

Don't underestimate the importance of cemeteries and houses of worship, two entities that represent the most significant dimensions of our ancestors' lives. Your search with your children might include photographing churches in which past generations were married. If you want to learn more about your great-aunt, spend a Sunday morning at the church she attended and talk to long-time members. Chances are someone in the congregation will recall past members and may be willing to talk to a relative.

Many of the churches where our ancestors gathered are probably still standing, while schools have surely changed either through modernization or demolition. Neighborhoods change over time, but houses remain. In addition, many social clubs and fraternal organizations—the German Hall, the Masons, the local VFW Post, and others—may still be in operation and may allow access to old records.

Family History Centers and Libraries

Many record repositories and libraries contain collections of historical records that offer helpful information to family historians. These records give older children the opportunity to look at their heritage, and though often fragmentary, they can help fill the gaps in your family tree. Likewise, they can give your children a chance to experience the thrill of discovering new information about their ancestors. Making use of these records with your children is a lesson not only in family history, but also in research.

Create a health record for your family and involve your children. They can help review the causes of death listed on death certificates and research diseases that run in your family, keeping a chart of the illnesses they find.

As you work with your children to help them to understand your family history, make a game out of it. One mother helped introduce her child to microfilm in the Family History Center by telling her young daughter that she could see what had happened on the day she was born. Setting up the microfilm for a newspaper, the mother proceeded slowly, stopping occasionally to point out cartoons and other items that might be interesting to her daughter. When the father joined them some time later, the child proudly announced to him that she was finding out what had happened in the world on her birthday. The whole process hadn't taken more than fifteen minutes, but the mother's patience and creativity had helped to make it a positive experience for her daughter.

If your research involves talking to relatives, involve your children in the process. While younger children can become restless talking to elderly people they don't know, older children might be persuaded to see it as detective work.

Kids on the Internet

Children have taken to computers wholeheartedly, and it could be to your advantage to take their interest and combine it with family history research.

Because of the risks involved with children on the Internet, be sure that your child knows about computer safety. You might want to leave your family computer in a high-traffic area; discuss family computer rules so that your children know not to answer spam e-mail, or to give a website their full name, birth date, or social security number.

Your children can help you look online for pictures of the ships their immigrant ancestors traveled on.

Perhaps the best place for genealogists to begin is <www.familysearch.org>, the family history website for The Church of Jesus Christ of Latter-day Saints. Its searchable databases have over a billion names and the Pedigree Resource File has over 66 million names. With all these names, it's fairly certain that your child could enter the name of one of your ancestors and find clues to many more.

This is also a good opportunity to talk with your child about the importance of documentation and the community of genealogists who are all working on your family genealogy.

Because of the increasing popularity of genealogy and the growing numbers of young genealogists, you'll find several specialized genealogy websites just for kids. USGenWeb for Kids at <www.rootsweb.com/~usgwkidz/> and WorldGenWeb at <www.rootsweb.com/~wgwkids/> are two places to be sure to visit. Your children will find pedigree charts, family group sheets, and other forms to print out, as well as ideas for projects, suggestions for e-mail research, and lots of information on different countries. Sit down with your children and let them show you how capable they are with the computer.

Your children will also enjoy Genealogy Today Junior Edition at <http://genealogytoday.com/junior/index.html>. The articles are fun and engaging, and children will find an invitation to submit stories about ancestors and do surname searches.

Don't forget to check out the Ancestry World Tree at <www.ancestry.com> and RootsWeb at <www.rootsweb.com>. Your children may need some help navigating the riches of these resources, but it won't take them long to learn how to accurately search the databases and mailing lists for information on the family.

Your older children can scan photographs into a genealogical scrapbooking program. Photos on CD make great gifts for family members.

Cyndi's List at <www.cyndislist.com> includes a section for kids you may want to investigate. Also, preview categories such as maps and passenger ships to explore with your children. Cyndi's List also has a section for Ellis Island that your children will find interesting. While our ancestors may have landed at many different ports in America, it is estimated that 100 million Americans are directly related to immigrants who came through Ellis Island. Your children may enjoy looking for ancestors who came through New York between 1892 and 1924.

Similarly, Kinship Prints at <www.kinshipsprints.com> shows ships that were used from 1890 to 1940. Your children may enjoy seeing the ships their ancestors traveled on, particularly if they are able to find some journals kept by their ancestors or other passengers.

Remember to have your children keep a log of the websites they've visited so they don't duplicate their efforts later. An easy way to do this is to keep an open document in your word processing program and have them copy and paste the URL from the browser window and type the name of the website.

Stories from Relatives

While one aspect of family history research involves research with records and microfilm, another involves talking with people. Both are equally valuable. An important lesson for genealogists of all ages is the need to gain information from the living while they can, information that might not be so readily available later. However, if there is a chance that sensitive information will be shared, it may be better to involve the children in other aspects of family history at this time.

Arrange a photograph album by theme. Keep all pictures for holidays or birthdays over the years together. Your children will enjoy seeing how holidays were celebrated in past years.

One woman found that when her children asked her parents for stories about their childhood, the parents were much more likely to respond in detail, especially when the stories were needed for school projects and scouting merit badges. Often the questions were asked through e-mail and the parents wrote lengthy responses, which could then be cut and pasted into a permanent family history. Others have noticed and reported a similar phenomenon: that grandchildren and grandparents are often able to communicate more freely than parent and child. If this is the case, allow the next generation to ask the questions during an interview.

Sandra Cook, who lives in the area where both of her parents were born and raised, has been sharing her family history with her children for many years. Sandra always makes a point of speaking with people who appear to be of her parents' generation, and her example has taught her children not to be embarrassed to talk to people who may have information about the family.

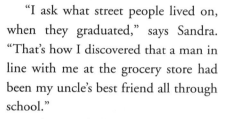

Put together a time capsule of goals, pictures, memorabilia, and a list of favorite things to be opened in five years. Your children will love to put it together and will enjoy reminiscing about the past when it is opened.

"I ask what street people lived on, when they graduated," says Sandra. "That's how I discovered that a man in line with me at the grocery store had been my uncle's best friend all through school."

Help your children open the lines of communication with elderly relatives. The stories that these relatives can share may be your children's best and strongest link to their ancestors.

Your own family can tell you things you never suspected—that your dad once played bugle, banjo, and harmonica and marched in parades with the Red Devils Drum and Bugle Corps. His mother, on the other hand, is more likely to recall your dad's sledding accident when stones became embedded in his face, an occasion that made her pass out.

When children take part in research by helping you collect stories from elderly relatives, they learn two other important lessons: 1) respect for the accomplishments and struggles of their elders, and 2) valuable interviewing skills. Help your children to understand that the stories their elderly relatives have to share are their best connection to the past. Encourage them to participate in collecting and recording these stories.

If you spent your childhood in the same area in which you are raising your family, you will have certain advantages in sharing your past with your children. Take them to the pagoda in the city park where your husband proposed to you. Show them the bridge by the mill on Main Street where everyone in town used to meet. Although the area today may be frequently deserted on weekends, you might tell your children, "When we were young the bridge was so packed on a Saturday night you could hardly get through." This easy proximity to places of significance is a great advantage since you can introduce your children to places and people of your past.

Family Reunions

Take advantage of opportunities to introduce your children to their relatives whenever possible—at holidays, weddings, reunions, birthdays, and other family occasions. Such encounters will help them develop a curiosity about their family history as they get to know their relatives through shared interests such as sports, hobbies, and other interests that run in your family. Children may even develop close friendships with relatives that can last a lifetime.

Before a family reunion, encourage your older children to write to their distant cousins. This will help ease the process of getting acquainted.

To make a reunion experience a positive one for children, some advance planning is necessary, whether you are hosting the reunion or simply attending it. In any large gathering, children tend to get neglected since adults are often busy attending to the details. But with a little effort, you can make reunions more enjoyable for the children who attend. "Plan your reunion around your kids," advises Bonnie Cameron Laliberte. "If the kids are having fun, the adults will have fun as well."

In many cases, family gatherings and reunions may not be the best place to spark children's interest in family history. Children are rarely physically or mentally in tune with adults and elderly relatives sitting around telling stories about the good old days. On the other hand, if the reunion has some activities for the children, it could be a wonderful opportunity for children to become excited about the past. For example, since children respond best to special, private time with close family members, such as grandparents, aunts, and uncles, you might plan an activity where children could explore a trunk or suitcase filled with family "treasures" while an older family member supervises and tells stories about each item. Children could even visit with a favorite aunt or uncle and look at family photographs together.

A memory matching game involving pictures of ancestors is another way to give children an introduction to family history that is more suitable to their age. You could play a form of "To Tell the Truth" where the children guess which adults are telling the truth about an episode from their past. Both children and adults may also enjoy games that the grandparents played as children. There are many activities that will help build relationships, whether you hold your event outdoors on a sunny summer afternoon or on a fall evening with hot chocolate by the fireside. Other fun activities include old-fashioned cooking projects such as churning butter or making ice cream, quilting, hiking, and storytelling.

Depending on the ages of the children in your family, you may want to divide the children into two groups to accommodate their different interests and abilities.

Scrapbooks and Photograph Albums

Whether you choose to call it a scrapbook or legacy book, or whether you use a photograph album or a simple loose-leaf binder, all are appropriate ways to capture your family's legacy. Each serves a different function, but all can play a useful role in capturing your family history and the memories you would like to preserve.

Scrapbooks were originally just that—books of Victorian scraps in the nineteenth century. They often held paper lace cutouts, pressed flowers, postcards, and other items of interest to their owner. Today, a scrapbook for your daughter might contain drawings she did in preschool, photos of her soccer team from the local paper, Mother's Day cards in which she signed her name, or samples of her school work from kindergarten.

Legacy books tend to be focused on the history of the family. They might contain photocopied portraits of ancestors with dates and places of birth, death, and marriage, information about siblings, and facts about their lives. The level of sophistication depends on the skill and time the creator has to put into the book.

Some creative parents have encouraged their children to include written reflections in their photograph albums. Other parents find that loose-leaf binders work perfectly to hold documents that are letter-sized, made of construction paper, or too bulky to fit into a flat scrapbook. Still other parents prefer a scrap box for larger objects. A combination of these often works best.

A scrapbook is a wonderful way to involve children actively in their genealogy. Let your child assemble your family history into an organized book of presentation quality. (Your children might be more computer literate than you are anyway, or if they aren't, you may want them to be.) Good, well-documented research captured in family charts on computer and double-checked for accuracy can produce a wonderful gift that relatives will treasure. Even a simple version of your family history as far back as it has been traced can be photocopied and stapled together between a front and back cover as a gift for family members.

Keep a scrapbook or scrap box, depending on the size of the items, with your children's favorite school projects. Since it's impossible to keep them all, select those that are most special. For some items, it may be enough to take a picture of it and include that in your scrapbook. A good rule is "Display the best, dispense with the rest." Make one scrapbook collection from your own childhood, your mother's, your grandmother's, or your great-aunt's. Share these with your children. It will give them a sense of belonging, of having a special place in the family that is uniquely theirs.

My daughter created pages of red, white, and blue construction paper on which she glued mementos from the last Memorial Day parade. There were newspaper photos and clippings about the weather plus some candy wrappers that had held little treats tossed by those riding on the floats.

Assemble a treasure box to serve as a place to keep various items that are special to your children. You might include a postcard, a favorite book, even a childhood birthstone given by a grandmother.

Buy your children a photograph album of their own and give them a disposable camera so they can start developing an eye for visual images now. Later on you may want to invest in a nicer camera for the older children who take the project seriously. They will learn to value photographs and the memories that go with them. As the years pass, they will enjoy looking back at their photos and remembering the moments and the people who inspired them.

Vanessa Cumming created a family book with photocopied pictures of each family member to teach her children about their family history. The pages opposite the photos contain basic information identifying the ancestors and their relationship to the current generation. Copies were distributed to other relatives as well. Because it is printed on inexpensive paper, Vanessa can introduce her two-year-old to his ancestors. (Spills and tears aren't critical to a copy that is stored on a CD and can be easily reprinted.)

A family genealogy assembled in book form is far more likely to be taken seriously and treasured as opposed to notes that can easily get lost. A scrapbook that is well put-together is much more attractive than a box of loose, messy papers.

Don't worry that you aren't done with your research or that you could include more if you had time. Family history is ongoing, and the book captures a moment in time. Your children will be able to help you fill in the rest—and the point of tracing your family history is to pass it on to descendants who care about their legacy.

Give your children a disposable camera and let them choose their own subjects. In the years to come, their photo albums will show their unique personalities.

You may also want to start a baby book for each child, regardless of age. Get those newspaper clippings and kindergarten drawings into a permanent format before more time passes. My daughter's scrapbook holds small treasures from her kindergarten days when she used to bring home scraps of paper with friends' telephone numbers scribbled on them, some barely readable but always heartwarming.

Perhaps you still have the baby books you received when your son was an infant, and they are on a shelf or in a box, unused or incomplete and forgotten. If you are starting fresh, begin with your child's current interests: school, hobbies, goals, and friends. You can always go back and fill in the earlier years as items from those days surface or are remembered.

Chapter Five

Writing That Connects Lives

As you think back over the lives of your children, you may be surprised at the realization of how many written sources exist that contain information about them—the newspaper clippings from school and soccer games tucked inside shoeboxes and drawers, the autograph books from childhood, the high school yearbooks showing their friends and interests. It would be nearly impossible to count the letters and birthday cards from friends and relatives containing affectionate, often personal notes that are proof of valued relationships and special days.

In this same way, old letters, yearbooks, and other artifacts from earlier generations can give your children insights into the lives, thoughts, and emotions of their ancestors. Old yearbooks belonging to relatives and family members may contain titles such as Most Popular, Most Intelligent, or Most Likely to Succeed—which can tell quite a bit about relatives who don't like to brag. Your son might be amazed to discover that his dad was voted Most Artistic in his senior year in high school, while the moniker Class Clown reveals an altogether different aspect of his personality. A grandfather's letters can contain pet names and expressions, perhaps even poetry, that may show a well-concealed tender heart.

"Although my father was thoughtful and introspective all his life, I did not often see him with a book," says Anna Lindsey. "Yet after his death I found poems written in his handwriting on philosophical and spiritual topics like self-awareness tucked in his bureau drawer and in his wallet. The influence of these writings lives on as a testament to his philosophies and values."

Help your children to begin now to create and collect these valuable written records that will give meaning to their lives and to others in the years to come.

E-mails to Grandma

Because of the daunting distances that can separate brothers, sisters, cousins, aunts and uncles, grandparents, and grandchildren these days, families are finding innovative ways to keep in touch. Rather than allowing themselves to dwell on the separation, they use technology to keep the family close.

Help your young children write postcards or letters to grandparents or other relatives who would appreciate hearing from them.

Keeping in touch by e-mail is just one way to span the miles between families. Its speed and convenience have made it a popular method of communication. Our ability to scan photos and send clever online cards and sound files combine to make e-mail an increasingly personal form of communication.

But e-mail is only one of the options for communication available to us today. Mary Allard, an imaginative and determined grandmother, bought two fax machines—one for herself and one for her son's family.

Now she can send notes, mazes, riddles, and pages from coloring books for her grandchildren to color. The children happily fax their artwork to her in return. Her children enjoy hearing from her and receiving something by fax addressed to them.

Some grandparents record themselves reading a book on audiotape or video. Sending a tape and book to the grandchildren is a gift that comes complete with Grandma's voice. This is also a good way to prepare children to meet relatives for the first time or to help long-distance families keep in touch. That way, when young children see their grandparents again after a long separation, voices and faces are dear and familiar.

Combining the benefits of digital cameras and e-mail allows families to share holiday festivities as well. Grandparents can watch their grandchildren opening presents on Christmas Day only minutes later and feel they are still a part of the lives of their faraway children and grandchildren. Rent or buy a video camera and make your own video to send your "presence" to the television set of absent relatives. But don't wait for special occasions and holidays. Any family gathering can be an excuse to prepare a message for other family members living outside the area.

Children who have learned to write can keep a family diary for a vacation or keep minutes of family meetings.

If you have been meaning to keep in touch with relatives out of state, make an audiotape with family news updates as a spontaneous or a seasonal gift for relatives. Don't rely on holidays as an excuse to bring them up to date on your life and activities. By then you will have forgotten the cute remark your three-year-old made in church last Sunday. If your children are expressive, let them record the audiotapes. Be creative; help them set events to appropriate music.

Before the advent of videotaping, my aunt used to take advantage of family gatherings to record people's thoughts and moods. The audiotape would include a current report on the status of the family (everyone was encouraged to speak into the microphone), and occasionally a tape would feature singing by any child who was willing. The tapes were made on the East Coast and sent to West Coast relatives so they would know what was going on with the rest of the family.

Letter Writing

Of all the mail that arrives daily, almost nothing is more appreciated than a letter from a relative or friend. Even a brief sincere note or card serves as a reminder of a familial connection. Encouraging your children to write to relatives is a positive way to build a solid bond with family members far away.

You can help your children revive the art of letter writing using these few simple steps to make their letters to relatives more appealing. First, make the letters personal. Suggest that your children include unique things about themselves in their letters. Your son might include that he has been playing the harmonica since he was three and that his sheep took first prize at a county fair. Your daughter could say that summer vacation is her favorite time of year and her favorite food is fresh strawberries from the garden.

Second, help your children personalize their letters as much as possible for the person they are writing. Have them ask about family members, work, school, and their interests. Explain to your children that some people might have mixed emotions about their past. They may have lost loved ones or become separated from them over meaningless feuds; no doubt there are events they would rather forget. If your children are seeking information about their family history, help them to be sensitive in their inquiries.

Third, as you help your children personalize their letters, try to make yourself and your child aware ahead of time of any major life events, illnesses, or traumas that relatives might have experienced recently. Encourage your children to show a genuine interest and concern for the individual to whom they write. Sincerity shines through.

Fourth, help your children to make their letters engaging, humorous, and fun to read. Your own knowledge of your family and your experiences will help you to do this.

You can help your children have a more positive experience by reminding them to be personal and pleasant in their introductory letter (and in follow-up letters as well, of course). Be sure they let the recipient know that the writer is interested in family history and in getting to know members of the family better. Genealogy is a popular hobby, and recipients shouldn't be too surprised by this.

Handwritten letters are more time-consuming than a letter written on a computer, but many people still prefer the handwritten letter and feel it is more personal. The choice to use attractive stationery also shows that the sender cares about the letter's appearance.

> **Older children might enjoy creating a timeline of their life, beginning with their birth and going through their childhood and teen years. They might want to include details about friends, learning experiences, and hobbies.**

Encourage your child to keep the correspondence going once it has been initiated. Corresponding by mail often leads to enduring, meaningful friendships and enriching relationships that can sustain a person in need of emotional support.

Jennifer Gibson has been writing to her cousins in Switzerland for nearly twenty years. Her American uncle married a woman from abroad and moved to Geneva, where he raised his family. Jennifer's mother felt it was important for the family to keep in touch with relatives, so she asked ten-year-old Jennifer to write

to them. At the time Jennifer resisted the idea. "I knew them all," she recalls. "They came back to the States every year. But I didn't know what to say to them."

Still, her mother wanted her to write, so Jennifer started writing her cousins every Christmas and once during the year. Exchanging letters allowed her to grow up with them and to savor significant changes in their lives. Now, two decades later, Jennifer is grateful her mother insisted upon the correspondence.

"We're closer than we would have been otherwise," she says. "We get along better now that we're older."

Put together a brief family history. Dad and Mom can write a summary of their birth, childhood, school years, and courtship. Children can also write a summary of their lives to that point. Add photos and place the pages in archival-quality sheets and binders.

Since her cousins have children who are close to her daughter's and son's ages, Jennifer hopes the next generation will also maintain the family connection.

Fun with Pen Pals

Do you have an older child who would benefit from having a pen pal? Some of the best pen pals might lie within your own family, either in the United States or overseas.

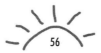

While it might sound strange, you may even find some potential pen pals in the obituaries of family members. For example, your great-grandfather's obituary will probably list some of his brothers or sisters who are still alive, either in the United States or in the old country. If they are living abroad, the inclusion of their names in the obituary may mean that the family was still in touch with them at the time of his death. This could be your opportunity to establish a relationship with these relatives. Perhaps they married and had children, and your family has new relatives in the old country and now have children who would be interested in having a pen pal across the ocean.

Sometimes e-mail is the best chance for teenage cousins who live in different states to get to know each other. As a parent, you might want to initiate contact with another parent to ease the way for your children to communicate and develop a friendship.

Discovering relatives in other regions with whom you share a bloodline also offers the possibility of new relationships. Some children might enjoy helping you trace an ancestor's descendants on foreign soil, filling in the family tree up to the present. Others may just want to get the name and address of a cousin in Ireland so they can write their first letter right away. Count either way as a success.

Have young children describe themselves using words that begin with the letters of their name.

Family Newsletters

Family newsletters let you stay in touch with relatives in other areas of the world by sharing news on a regular basis. Since communication is vital to keeping long-distance relationships alive, consider creating a family newsletter for an occasion other than Christmas.

Involve your children in the process of creating and sending out your newsletter. It's a great way to help your children become even more computer literate than they already are. You might include an interview with the local family matriarch or an article about an ancestor's profession, home, or country. Older children could even research and write this type of article, which could appear with a byline and a picture.

Desktop publishing programs make it easy to produce an attractive, appealing newsletter. Your children can help in many ways. There are many clip-art graphics available to choose from. Use headings and categories to highlight special events, activities, accomplishments, birthdays, and other dates to remember. Make your newsletter fun and creative.

Preparing the newsletter will provide many additional benefits for your children as well. Typing up the information and laying it out on the computer will expose them to both genealogy and computer technology. They'll soon realize that their ancestors were more interesting than they could ever have imagined.

Diaries

For many years, keeping a diary has been seen as the province of little girls, but the world owes much to the diaries of great men and women. Give diaries as birthday gifts to all of your children with a lesson on how to use them. Sit down with each child for a few minutes in the evening and talk about the events of the day and what your child might write about. When your children are too little to write for themselves, keep a diary or journal for them so they will have a record of the early events in their lives. One mother records her children's unique phrases and activities in her computer journal. "I'm too busy with two children and working to keep a journal by hand," she says. "While I'd rather have it in my own handwriting, I work on the computer every day. If I keep a journal for my children on my computer, I know the important moments will be recorded."

A family diary for special occasions can also preserve those memories. The next time your family takes a vacation or goes on a camping trip, keep a diary. A vacation diary can be supplemented with photographs when the pictures have been developed. Identifying people and places is much easier when done this way.

Another good time for diary-keeping might be in the month before a new brother or sister is added to the family. An older child could be the scribe, or the assignment could rotate to a new scribe each week. Younger children could dictate while parents write, giving them a chance to voice feelings about the new baby or about other accomplishments and activities.

Chapter Six

Fun on the Road

For the vast majority of family historians, especially those with young children, attending to the needs of children is often so demanding that there is little time left to spend on family history. However, with some forethought and planning, you can find inventive ways to take your children with you on your excursions. The family that travels with a genealogical intent has the opportunity to visit cemeteries, churches, and workplaces associated with ancestors. This can give children an unforgettable encounter with their family's unique past as they see firsthand the birthplaces and towns where their ancestors were born and raised. If you plan to visit relatives or attend a family reunion, your family may be able to meet some relatives for the first time, renew acquaintances with other relatives, and even establish new relationships that may endure throughout their lifetimes.

Travel requires considerable planning and attention to detail beforehand, and endurance, flexibility, and patience during the trip. Because of this your children should ideally be old enough to appreciate the sights and experiences of new places. Careful consideration of the ages and personalities of your children will help you determine when to plan such a major trip. The benefit of bringing children along is that they will see firsthand how important their family history is to you. While your children might get restless and bored, involving them in the process—while including extra time for breaks and stops along the way—can also make your visit fun and adventurous for them.

Make the most of opportunities in your own region of the country. Start with shorter trips to cemeteries, museums, historical houses, and other sites in your area. Before you travel, do your homework with your children. Consult library books for historical milestones that occurred during the course of your ancestors' lives. Get an atlas and show your children where they will be traveling, especially if the distance is great. Whether your travel is local or in another region of the country, sit down with your children and consider the distances on a map. In combination with a globe, this will help give children a sense of how far away their ancestors lived or, in the case of immigrants, how far their ancestors traveled to reach the New World.

Remember that this is a trip for your children as well. They should be able to get the maximum impact from the experience. Before you travel, have your children make a list of special things they'd like to see that are connected in some way with their ancestry. They can also look up the towns in which their ancestors were born, the churches in which they were married, and the cemeteries where they are buried.

As you plan for your genealogical trip, hold a family meeting to generate questions about ancestors you hope to find answers for on your travels. Assign an older child to take notes of these questions or to type up your notes on the computer. As clear as the questions may be before your trip, your memory will likely be occupied with travel-related concerns while you're away from home.

Keep a log of things you want to accomplish on your visit or trip. The children can help you by keeping your "to-do" lists of ancestors' graves you plan to visit, the addresses of significant buildings and historical sites, living relatives you hope to meet, and particular things you'd like to do in a given area.

Among other things on your list, you'll want to bring your camera and extra film, genealogy notes with pertinent information, and a pad and pencil to write with. If you're visiting relatives, you might want to bring copies of photographs to show them or to have them identify. But leave the originals at home.

Genealogy-oriented travel means an additional list of things to pack that other travelers would never miss. When a family historian travels, however, even if it's around the corner to visit Great-Aunt Martha, you want to go armed with the things you'll need to get the most out of your visit. Create the list with your children and let them offer suggestions.

Children's Museums

With hands-on displays and changing exhibits, museums always feature something new for children. Museums, particularly those that focus on local history, are likely to contain something of interest to your children that can be related to your own family history. When you take your children, connect the visit as much as possible to the history of your family.

In patching together a picture of your ancestors' lives, show your children elements of ordinary life. Begin with the general stuff of life—kitchen utensils, furniture, and clothes—and then fill in the background for your children.

Antique toy museums, some specializing in dolls or trains, provide a great opportunity for children to see the playthings that amused children in other centuries. Old-fashioned toys reveal both similarities and differences between children today and children of the past. One children's museum hosts a program of Mexican dancing by children affiliated with the state's Mexican organization. Children of many cultures can relate to dancing, dressing up, and having fun. The event is a festive occasion for all attendees, regardless of ethnic background.

Museums with exhibits that are specifically geared for youngsters can help your children visualize other periods in history. Seek out local museums at home and while your family is traveling. This will help open new worlds to your children.

Historic Museums and Homes

Your local historical museum is a wonderful place to begin a child's study of history and your family's history. If your family has lived in the area for several decades, the items in the museum will have even greater meaning because of their relevance to the lives of your ancestors.

All over the United States, you will find museums that focus on the unique cultural heritage of the region. These museums represent the lives of millions of immigrants in cities and towns across America. Photographs of people, firemen's uniforms, pictures of parades, newspaper clippings of important historical events, and the mementos of veterans all bring excitement about the past that textbooks can't capture.

When traveling, tell family stories to help pass the time, but when your voices give out, it's time for books on tape and music. Headphones and a battery-operated tape deck or CD player may be sufficient, unless your vehicle is equipped with a VCR.

The Museum of Work and Culture in Woonsocket, Rhode Island, is an interactive museum concentrating on the French Canadians who left the farms of Quebec for the factories of New England. Visitors can view the lives of a typical family from their roots in a Quebec farmhouse through their days as working immigrants. The museum highlights the cultural preservation of the language and customs of the French

Canadians and includes displays that focus on labor, immigration, and enterprise in the area. And your children will see firsthand how children in the past lived, worked, and played.

The thirty-seven reconstructed homes and community buildings of Vermont's Shelburne Museum, set on forty-five country acres, show in vivid detail many aspects of the lives of ordinary people from history. Shelburne is a delight for children, with a Circus Building that contains a complete carousel and a 500-foot-long miniature circus parade. Other exhibits are equally impressive. The Horseshoe Barn, an enormous horseshoe-shaped dairy barn, contains nearly two hundred antique carriages, wagons, sleighs, coaches, fire trucks, and other vehicles.

Shelburne also features an elegant luxury railroad car with a mahogany-paneled parlor and velvet furnishings, a jail from 1890 made of slate reinforced with railroad irons that was in use for fifty years, a Greek Revival home from 1832, and a saltbox from 1782. An apothecary shop, toyshop, Stagecoach Inn, meeting house, and gallery also grace the expansive grounds. There is even a four-bedroom lighthouse from 1871 that served as home and workplace for eleven lighthouse keepers and their families.

Museums that collect, preserve, research, and interpret a city's history can be a source of delight and discovery to children. If your great-great-grandfather was a clockmaker when he emigrated from Switzerland,

Bring along a thumbnail sketch of your family history with names, dates, and birthplaces when your travel. (You might even assign one of your children to be the "expert" on a particular ancestor.) Also, bring a copy of the family history notes you've prepared to leave with your relatives. They'll be grateful you're sharing with them what you have already learned about your relatives, both living and dead.

visit a clock museum. The setting alone will give your children a feeling for what it may have been like to work as a clockmaker.

Try a folk art museum or other specialized museum if you want to capture the feel of the past for your child. Explore the territories inhabited by your ancestors for museums that will give them a feel for their era.

Some cities offer an annual festival in which historic homes are open to public view and their contents and other memorabilia are on display. Many communities also have historic homes that are open regularly, while some homes are open to the public on special occasions like Christmas. Historic homes may feature artifacts such as spinning wheels or weaving looms, original or restored period furnishings, stenciled walls, or antiques that include colonial pewter and quaint needlework samplers. Your children will feel that they have stepped into the past.

You will find beautifully restored homes for authors such as Mark Twain, whose boyhood home in Hannibal, Missouri, can be visited, and Louisa May Alcott, whose book *Little Women* was set at Orchard House in Concord, Massachusetts. Fruitlands, Louisa's father's experimental attempt at utopian living in Harvard, Massachusetts, is also open to visitors. Here the public is given an intimate view of how the inhabitants lived along with a chance to see the clothing they wore, personal belongings such as diaries or cross-stitch samplers, and the bedrooms recreated as they were in the Alcotts' day. If your daughters are fans of *Little Women,* they can imagine growing up in this environment and writing, sewing by the fire during the winter, and reading by lamplight.

The fact that the eastern part of America is filled with Victorian three-story tenement houses means that many of the homes inhabited by our ancestors still exist. These houses were often shared by family members who lived in an age in which the first priority was to take care of family. This meant that apartments were frequently rented out to relatives newly arrived in America or to sons or daughters and their children, which explains why children of earlier generations knew their grandparents so well. Often they grew up in the same house, sometimes on the same floor.

If your ancestors live in towns that are half a day's journey or so from where you reside, plan a brief visit to drive by their homes and photograph them. It will give you a clearer context in which to place them and to imagine their daily lives. If relatives know their street addresses, it will save you time. If they don't, it might be worth your while to take a day or two to visit the town so you can find the homes.

The experience will be unforgettable for your children if you have prepared them for such an event. Seeing the homes will also give you a chance to absorb the flavor of the neighborhood as you try to imagine what it was like in your great-grandfather's day.

Renaissance Fairs and the SCA

Even if you haven't traced your ancestors back to the Middle Ages, Renaissance fairs are a great way to give your children a historical experience and provide a day of fun and entertainment for all. The festive spirit of celebrating so commonly associated with the Middle Ages is present in all its glory here.

While some of the appeal is fantasy, the concept is a great hook for children, giving them a chance to dress up in medieval costumes, brandish a sword, and eat foods such as a leg of fowl. Among the highlights of King Richard's Faire in South Carver, Massachusetts, are vendors' booths filled with crafts that include medieval headgear, jewelry, cloaks, weaponry, statuary, fortune telling, and much more. Renaissance fairs are held across America as well as abroad.

The dancing, costumes, food, jousting, and theatricals add to the atmosphere of merrymaking. The day of historical fun is punctuated by encounters with people in character, making it that much easier to imagine how our medieval ancestors might have looked and acted.

Renaissance fairs represent an exciting way to introduce children to an era that is completely different from theirs.

You needn't be descended from a king or queen to benefit from attending a Renaissance fair. In addition to all the fun you and your children will have, the historical ambiance will create a feeling about the past they likely won't forget.

For older children who are a bit more fanciful, the Society for Creative Anachronism (SCA) might be for them. Forget the cholera and the bloody battles for a moment, and picture instead the romantic side of the medieval period, with all the fantasy and lore of its legends. Founded in 1966, the Society for Creative Anachronism researches and re-creates European history before 1600. The SCA has seventeen kingdoms (or regional chapters) throughout the world.

The SCA website at <www.sca.org> has links to the individual website for whatever kingdom is closest to you. The Kingdom of Atenveldt, for example, is the state of Arizona. The Kingdom of Calontir is comprised of Kansas, Missouri, Iowa, Nebraska, and Northern Arkansas. Each website gives dates for events and membership information, describes the activities planned, and lists contact information.

The SCA recreates the crafts, sciences, arts, traditions, and literature of the Middle Ages. Activities include calligraphy, dance, martial arts, metalwork, cooking, stained glass, and costuming.

A participant in the Society for over twenty years, Gail Eastwood Stokes says her sons have grown up with SCA. Many summers during their childhood they participated in the mid-August revelry known as Pennsic at the annual camping event in Slippery Rock, Pennsylvania. Gail feels SCA activities offer a wonderful creative outlet for children.

"My older son was introduced to archery through SCA," she says. "He was able to use those skills later when he was appointed director of our YMCA's archery program and became licensed to teach. SCA provided the foundation." She added that her sister found encouragement for her artistic talent through SCA. Through the Society she found an opportunity to use her skills in calligraphy and illumination, leading to a successful career in commercial calligraphy.

Older children can choose to design and construct costumes or to make armor, weapons, and shields, and then wear them to learn how it feels to wear armor in combat. Events vary by season and often feature tournaments, art exhibits, workshops in medieval practices, and an evening feast with dancing. Members are expected to choose a name to use in the Society, such as John of Wardcliff, or they may even devise something more elaborate and Gaelic-sounding, like Oisin Dubh mac Lochlainn.

Families willing to travel can find activities every weekend if they have the energy. One weekend may feature a medieval feast; the following weekend there might be a joust in a neighboring state; and the next weekend might include a medieval dance. A sampling of events include New York's Crystal Snowflake Ball, Pennsylvania's Games and Galliards VIII, and Connecticut's Fooles Feast. A Twelfth Night feast held several years ago was based on historical customs and included period games for youngsters.

While many people are involved in both SCA and Civil War reenacting, authenticity is not the primary goal of SCA. Participants in the Society refer to themselves as "re-creationists" since they do not usually reenact particular moments from history. Since the medieval period is harder to document, this is an additional element of fantasy in re-creating events. There is much that is authentic, however. For people with interests in historic costuming, Elizabethan or Renaissance country dancing, and fencing, there is a great deal they can learn.

The martial arts play a large role in SCA and are among the most popular demonstrations given by recreationists at elementary schools, using weapons made of rattan that are sized and weighted to be authentic. The martial arts are done as a sport, and SCA requires that children learn it and be certified to perform it. Safety regulations restrict fencing to those eighteen years and older, but children can begin training before they turn eighteen.

Historic USA

No matter what part of the United States became a permanent home for your ancestors, museums and historical exhibits of importance to family historians are spread across the country from the Atlantic to the Pacific. Children's and specialty museums such as train or sports memorabilia museums, are especially effective in introducing children to the past. Because many historic sites, museums, and historical societies maintain websites, it is possible to use the Internet to do research before leaving home so you can target the areas you want to take your children.

When traveling to historic sites in the United States, give each child a map with your route highlighted in bright colors. It will allow your children to chart their progress and give them a sense of how far they are traveling from home.

Each region offers a different picture in the jigsaw puzzle that represents the colonization of America. It is significant that America, the "melting pot," was colonized in its early days not only by England but also by France, Spain, Russia, and the Netherlands. Before the English set foot in Jamestown, the Southwest was colonized by the Spanish. Immigrants of many nationalities including those from Europe lost their lives at the Alamo.

French settlements formed a continuous band from Louisiana to Vermont. The Great Lakes region was settled by Scandinavians while Native Americans of various tribes appeared in all areas. African-Americans were among the earliest to arrive as slaves, on both the east and west coasts. Millions of immigrants arrived at New York's Ellis Island during its years of operation, far more than to any other American port.

Although we rely on ancestral records for knowledge of our forebears, living history is everywhere. Places that bring history to life connect us with the past in a vibrant, immediate way that can only be fully appreciated by being there. These kinds of places are especially appropriate for children because they reveal the past in realistic, imaginative ways.

New England and the East. On the East Coast, historical sites offer excellent opportunities to expose children to history in many of the places where their ancestors' American experiences began. If your children are descended from America's early settlers, these sites might correlate with their own family history. For those with ancestors in seventeenth-century New England, these are ideal places to bring your family. Here history is in the air, and it is easy to imagine walking in our forefathers' footsteps.

At Old Sturbridge Village in Massachusetts, characters in period costumes will wave to you from ox-drawn carts in summer and nod to you on the snow-covered common in winter. Historic interpreters at this re-created early nineteenth-century village work in a general store, a tin shop, a livestock pound, a gristmill, a blacksmith shop, a one-room schoolhouse, a working farm, and various furnished homes. They also participate in seasonal exhibits that include sheep shearing and maple sugaring. Children can join the Old Sturbridge Village Kids Club, which offers a newsletter and monthly activities, History Mystery quizzes, drawings, contests, and craft projects. Its website at <www.osv.org> has a Fun and Games page that includes Nine-Men's Morris, one of the world's oldest games of strategy, and Fox and Geese, brought to America by French and Hessian troops during the Revolutionary War. It also contains puzzles and other activities.

Mystic Seaport in Connecticut, a picturesque re-created nineteenth-century port, is home to a shipyard with working craft shops and square-rigged sloops and schooners along its shores. You can smell the salt air as you pass Fishtown Chapel, the ship carver's shop, the Custom House, the ship chandlery, and the Spouter Tavern. Visitors can stroll through an heirloom garden with flowers of a hundred years ago, hear a sea captain's wife recount her travels at the American Seaman's Friend Society, or tour the training ship *Joseph Conrad*. Your children will find it easy to imagine what sailing life was like when they climb on board the *Charles W. Morgan*, a whale ship built in 1841. They can even join in the choruses of work songs as they watch the staff and adult visitors hoist the sails.

Assign one of your children to be "keeper of the camera." Take pictures of everything that has a connection to your family—relatives, ancestral homes, churches, gravestones.

Based on records, journals, and archeological findings, Plimoth Plantation is a reproduction of a Massachusetts pilgrim village from 1627. Costumed villagers in thatched houses dine on early-American fare and share stories about all aspects of life from their wardrobe to their professions. Educational programs have focused on arms and armor, seventeenth-century navigation, and religion among the colonists, and these are sure to entertain and educate your children. Typical activities might include family games that gave colonial children a respite from their chores, music and dances that were frowned on by Separatists, a visit with rare breed cows and goats in the barn, and cooking with Wampanoag clay corn pots.

Jamestown and Williamsburg, Virginia, are landmarks of Puritan and Colonial America; Williamsburg is as it appeared at the onset of the American Revolution. Character interpreters from drummers to balladeers transport visitors back in time in settings that include candlelight tours and authentic tavern dining. In Virginia, the Children's Museum of Richmond features hands-on exhibitions for youngsters. The Lewis and Clark exhibit allows children to build forts, use celestial navigation, and learn to identify animal tracks as Lewis and Clark did.

The South and the Midwest. The South features the Civil War battle sites of Bull Run, Shiloh, Appomattox, Cumberland Gap, and Vicksburg. Families looking for history related to the War of 1812 might consider New Orleans.

Heading west, Michigan's Frankenmuth Historical Museum explains how the town became "Michigan's Little Bavaria" and offers children's classes on topics such as pioneer living, German folk songs, and grandma's trunk, with toys and clothing to capture a child's fancy. Costumed interpreters at Living History Farms in Urbandale, Iowa, focus on the Midwest's agricultural heritage, performing the daily routines of Iowa's early residents in an outdoor museum that spans six hundred acres with a pioneer farming settlement and a Native American village from 1700.

For those of Scandinavian descent, the fact that the Vikings landed in Newfoundland means they left a trail. A rock in McAlester, Oklahoma, allegedly marks the southernmost point of their exploration. Anyone with Swedish or Norwegian ancestors might want to investigate to see what other bits of information they can dig up. They might also want to explore Seattle's Nordic Heritage Museum, the only museum in America to honor the accomplishments of Scandinavian immigrants.

The Midwest offers several museums of special interest to children. The Laura Ingalls Wilder Park and Museum in Burr Oak, Iowa, one of the childhood homes of the author of the *Little House* books, is a place children can relate to if they have ever read the books or watched reruns on television of *Little House on the Prairie*.

The West, the Northwest, and the Pacific Coast. The trail to the west left its mark all over America for children to see and relive vicariously. Fort Hays, in Kansas, is a frontier fort from 1865 that was built to protect railroad workers and travelers on Smoky Hill Trail. Children can't help but be enthralled as they walk in the footsteps of such legendary Westerners as General George Custer, Buffalo Bill Cody, and Wild Bill Hickok. In Missouri, Clark's Hill and Norton State Historic Site in Jefferson City is located on thirteen acres believed to be the hill William Clark climbed while camping at the mouth of the Osage River. When development is complete, visitors will be able to view much of the same landscape in Missouri as Clark did.

The settlers of the West and the men who laid the railroads left their mark as well. The Oregon Trail can still be seen along with monuments connected with the pioneers' travels. As an aid to prepare for your heritage vacation to this region, the Oregon-California Trails Association website at <www.octa-trails.org/home.asp> has information on the early settlers. Under Jumping off Today, a virtual tour button on the left brings up a map of the Oregon Trail. Your child will enjoy this interactive website, and it will prepare him or her for the visit.

The western region of the United States was for many the Promised Land, with the possibility of finding gold at the end of the journey. One trail website for children at <www.goldrushwagontrain.org> features a link to Wagon Train News that has photographs, journal entries, and stories from the trail. The link to events lets children see what happened to wagon trails along Gold Rush trails through Kansas, Colorado, Utah, Nevada, and California.

Some museums attempt to capture everyday life as it was and preserve it for our children. In Oregon, for instance, North Bend's Coos County Historical Society Museum features displays that include a 1900s parlor and a pioneer kitchen with exhibits on agriculture, logging, shipping, and mining. The Uppertown Firefighters Museum in Astoria contains firefighting equipment from 1877 to 1963 from the original fire station with hand-pulled, horse-drawn, and motorized fire engines. The Museum of Horse Drawn Vehicles in Oregon's Canyon City offers Old West displays, household and horse related trade goods, a general store, and display of over one hundred wagons, sleighs, and carriages.

Other Oregon museums focus on the occupations of the early settlers. The Chinese House Railroad Museum in Echo, Oregon, is located in a Chinese laborer bunkhouse from around 1883 and features railroad artifacts.

When travel isn't possible, you can still explore various regions of the country with your children on the Internet. Each state and many cities and counties maintain websites that offer a wealth of information. Many museums, historical societies, and countless organizations also host websites that may have online images, even virtual tours, in addition to information for the travelers and other interested parties.

Chapter Seven

The Importance of Traditions

When our immigrant ancestors came to America, they brought with them many traditions that they continued to observe in an attempt to retain some vestiges of their culture. Perhaps your family observes the German tradition of decorating with white lights at Christmas or the English tradition of gathering around the radio on Christmas Eve to hear Big Ben chime at midnight. Other traditions, such as St. Patrick's Day, have so evolved that they are celebrated with far more fervor in America than in the country of origin.

Traditions are important because of their value in creating a family connection for children. Your familiarity with Old World traditions can deepen your insight into your family's background and give your child an appreciation for cultural differences as well.

Local and Family Traditions

In June each year the Mather family celebrates its community's Old Home Days, an observance of the village's founding that includes a parade, library market day, a duck race in the local creek, a craft show, and more. They celebrate the Fourth of July with a family picnic at a state park. "For as long as I can remember we've done that," Lisa Mather says, "and there are pictures of me to prove it."

Celebrations that feature the same traditions each year become so sacred that families cannot imagine honoring them any other way. Long-held traditions increase in value as time goes on because many had their origins with our ancestors. You might be surprised to learn how long ago the customs your family observes today were actually started.

Many towns have places that served as gathering spots for those of previous generations. Anna Lindsay and her husband, although raised in different towns in neighboring states, discovered that both his parents and her mother had visited the same town park during their childhood each Christmas when the park was elaborately decorated. It was a revered holiday tradition for those of their generation who journeyed to see the sights year after year.

If such a gathering spot still exists, take your children there. Even if it has changed over time, your feelings about the place will be evident to your children and will communicate the significance and essence of the place to them.

The memory of routines helps to provide stability and comfort, as routines often do. Bonnie Cameron Laliberte has fond memories of Saturday mornings spent in her youth doing genealogical research with her mother, followed by tea and pastry in the afternoon. "Now that my mother is deceased, those memories have become even more special and uplifting," says Bonnie. "Now I try to carve out that special time with my own children."

Your family tradition might be a week's vacation in New York's Finger Lakes region every July. Or it could be something as simple as pizza and a movie every Friday night.

While not all holidays are celebrated to the same degree, most of them do involve traditions and the opportunity to meet with family. Tradition is the reason families pack up the station wagon and drive miles across the country to celebrate Thanksgiving and Christmas with family. Tradition is the reason for fireworks, for turkey at Thanksgiving, for picnics in the summer. Tradition is the reason many fire stations in the United States still keep Dalmatian dogs even though the fire wagons no longer have horses that require the presence of dogs to calm them. To many people, the concept of tradition explains why we continue to preserve traditions, even when they are not always convenient.

Have your children put together a collage of greeting cards from relatives to display during the holidays.

The role of traditions in a family is an important one. Traditions ground us in a familiar foundation and give us a comfortable space in which to grow, to live, and sometimes to die.

When a family member dies, a funeral can bring peace and closure. Similarly, since pets are often loved like a member of the family, children can be comforted by rituals that accompany the burial of a pet. Children can find solace when a pet is buried with a brief service, including a prayer and a few fond memories. Parents who begin such a tradition when their children are young help prepare them for other inevitable losses as they grow older.

Ethnic and Heritage Festivals

Many ethnic festivals are held in connection with holidays, such as St. Patrick Day (Irish), Cinco de Mayo (Hispanic), Dia de Camois (Portuguese), St. Joseph's Day (Italian), Dia de Portugal (Portuguese Independence Day), St. Jean de Baptiste (French), and Oktoberfest (German).

But many multicultural celebrations also occur independently of holidays. For example, the Siglo De Oro Drama Festival in El Paso, Texas, is held to celebrate the literary and linguistic ties still shared by Spain and the border region of Mexico and the United States. The festival brings together the best amateur and professional groups, presenting works of the Spanish masters. Participants come from as far away as Puerto Rico, Spain, and Jerusalem. The annual Greek Festival in Utah lasts three days every September, in honor of the Greek immigrants who worked in mines in the 1800s. In the small town of Midway, Utah, originally settled by Swiss immigrants, residents celebrate Swiss Days, and the arts and crafts fair draws larger crowds every year. Several states as well as Nova Scotia, Canada, hold Highland games annually as a reflection of those regions' Scottish population.

Create new family traditions, such as "Princess for a Day." Your daughter could choose her favorite meals to eat that day and help plan an activity for the whole family to participate in.

These activities bring communities and individuals together and celebrate the accomplishments of the country's early settlers. Talk with your children about the reasons for these celebrations, and when possible, take your children to enjoy the holiday activities that are specifically geared for families and young children.

Holiday Traditions

Sharing holiday traditions with your children is the link that creates a binding sense of family. On Christmas Eve, after my British grandparents had moved to America, they would visit a local town park decorated for the holidays. After seeing the lights they would return home for pie and coffee. They would take their customary seats in the rocking chairs that faced the fireplace with its electric logs, listen to the radio, and wait for Big Ben to chime midnight. "Ah, there it goes!" my grandfather would proclaim cheerfully year after year. I grew up hearing this story, how the familiar custom helped the family feel at home no matter where they were living.

Barbara Freshwater lives seven hundred miles from her children and grandchildren, so it is a special time for all when they gather on Christmas. "The children always love to see my tree," says Barbara. "It's decorated with the old German ornaments that were always on my mother's tree, and every Christmas I give a new ornament to each of my children."

Perhaps your idea of a celebration is to revive the exuberant Fourth of July parties that your ancestors celebrated with fireworks. One woman's great-grandmother and her six siblings were not only the children of a Civil War veteran but also Mayflower descendants, and as such they honored and esteemed their heritage all of their lives. For them the Fourth of July meant celebrating with fireworks set off from barrels in a sand lot across the street from their home.

Prepare a favorite family recipe for your children. Tell them where it came from and why it's your favorite.

Holiday Cooking

It is almost impossible to address holiday traditions without raising the issue of food. For some, no holiday celebration is complete without the special meals prepared that day. This is easily one aspect of family history with which children will be anxious to become involved. Holiday cooking serves to bring families together to share good food and conversation, and is perhaps the easiest and most enjoyable way to teach children about the importance of family and heritage.

Kathryn Edmonds learned to cook by watching her Lebanese mother prepare a variety of Mediterranean foods, like stuffed grape leaves or Tabouli. Kathryn recalls returning to the house after ice skating with her father and brothers and smelling the enticing scent of doughboys as she entered the front door. Several times a year her mother still makes Thi Tha Buns, a family favorite, and divides them among her children.

If you are a skillful seamstress, make an original costume or adapt an article of clothing to represent an ancestor your children admire.

"Our culinary heritage is very important," says Kathryn. "It is the basis not only for every holiday meal, but for most meals our family makes today."

Gail Brecher agrees that cooking is an important part of the holidays, and she comments that food plays a strong role particularly in the Jewish faith. "When you think of Jewish holidays your mouth almost waters at the thought of food because there are special dishes made only for these occasions," she says. "Every Friday night challah, wine, and chicken are consumed. Tradition is important and is observed through food. The particular dishes made at each holiday are symbolic. The round challah that is eaten in the fall represents an endless circle. In the Passover dinner, horseradish symbolizes the bitterness of slavery while the sweet greens, such as parsley, represent the sweetness of freedom. Matzoth, an unleavened bread, symbolizes the fact that there was no time to let the bread rise because the Jews were escaping from the Romans."

Cooking is a large part of Italian heritage as well. Italian heritage and family heritage are one and the same, says Audrey Loberti, wife and mother of a seven-year-old daughter. As a child, Audrey spent hours at the home of her grandmother. She remembers the small yard consumed by a sprawling vegetable garden that provided fresh vegetables all winter.

"My grandmother would cook, of course, and she would knit," says Audrey. "I was able to see it all firsthand and to hear about cousins and family my grandmother knew and remembered from Italy. Even as a child I was exposed to all kinds of dishes the family made."

Because eating and cooking were a big part of her heritage and upbringing, Audrey is passing these traditions on. "This is how my grandmother made it," she often tells her daughter, creating a bond between generations who will know each other only through shared customs and familiar objects.

Not only can children help in the kitchen to prepare dishes, add ingredients, and stir, they can also help put together recipe books by sending out letters to family members asking for favorite recipes as well as family stories and photographs to accompany the recipes. Letters should explain your plan to copy the recipes into a book and then make it available for distribution.

Louise Albanese collected over a hundred recipes that represented many branches of the family. "I was able to collect recipes from all sides of the family," she says. "Everyone was willing to share what they had, and it's treasured by everyone in our family. We have a large family that is scattered about the country, but most still manage to get together at holidays. Everyone has a favorite dish they make. Those were the recipes I compiled in our cookbook plus others handed down over the years. It represents a big part of our family history."

Family cookbooks need not be as large or comprehensive. Make yours unique to your family. Give it a title that reflects your heritage. Mine is entitled *Five Generations of Recipes: A Century of Tradition, 1888-1988*, and it contains twenty-two recipes that originated within our family. The book is a compilation of recipes from old and New England that were created up to four generations ago. Culled from kitchens in England and Scotland and from the Narragansett Indians, each recipe is attributed to an ancestor whose name, photograph, dates of birth and death, and country of origin are listed with it.

The recipes in Anna Lindsey's collection are mostly English and Scottish. They include directions on how to make plum pudding, steamed fig pudding, lemon cheese, and other old English specialties. Furthermore, she has a fun collection of cookie cutters for various holidays that helps to make holiday traditions with her children extra special.

Families are fortunate if their old recipes written on index cards have lasted, since they are often in the handwriting of the ancestors who introduced the dishes to the family.

Religious Traditions

In America, the immigrant experience and the religious experience are often inseparable since religion was what motivated millions of immigrants to leave their homelands and sail to America. The battles our ancestors waged against religious persecution and bigotry emphasize how important the First Amendment was to them with its guarantee to worship freely. The courage exhibited by our ancestors in such situations is a heritage our children and grandchildren can take pride in.

Many cultures are bound to previous generations by their faith. Those who suffered persecution because of their religion do not take the freedom to worship for granted, having endured great hardships in order to preserve their beliefs. If you have ancestors who immigrated to America for this reason, this is a tremendous heritage to share with your children. Talk with your children about the courage it takes to start over again in a new country and learn a new language—just for the chance to worship as they wish. You may even discuss what your lives would be like if your ancestors had not chosen to come to America.

Religious traditions are often a large part of American culture and values, so much so that they are almost inseparable from one another.

Thanksgiving, a uniquely American holiday, started as a Protestant celebration in which the Pilgrims would stand in church and state the blessings for which they were thankful. For those who celebrate Thanksgiving, this is a wonderful opportunity to share stories of our ancestors and express our appreciation for the choices and sacrifices they made that have given us so many freedoms today.

Having endured great persecution for their faith, Jews consider religious traditions an extremely important part of their heritage. Since Judaism depends on history for nearly all its traditions, tradition dictates what it is to be Jewish. The custom of naming children after a deceased ancestor builds an inherent connection with the past.

"Children are usually named after a relative who has passed on," says Gail Brecher, who converted to Judaism when she married her husband, Malcolm. "It is the Jewish name that carries on the tradition."

When a child is named for an ancestor, parents can talk to their child about his or her name, why they chose the name, and what they hope it would mean to their child.

Many religious traditions also provide a way for families to keep in contact with each other. Most members of the Strong family exchange Christmas cards to update one another. Martha Marble, secretary for the Strong family reunion, updates records on individual families. The Strong family has been holding their family reunion for more than 100 years, always on a Saturday. This is because Jacob Lane Strong, Sr., a religious man who believed in family and helping others, said, "You need to be in church on Sunday."

A great gift is a cookbook of family recipes. Include photos, stories, and countries of origin as you attribute the recipe to its creator. This project could be a fun family activity, and a good computer project for your child.

From a genealogical standpoint, religious traditions have had tremendous value to family historians because of the numerous church records available to them. According to Patrick M. Leehey, Research Director of Boston's Paul Revere Memorial Association, "Probably the most important effect religion has had on family history is simply that long before the government began keeping vital statistics on individuals and families, church records were kept, which today provide some of the most important sources of genealogical information about families."

Chapter Eight

Adopted Children: A Dual Heritage

Adoption is often serendipitous, as I learned after I adopted the first of two daughters from China. Although my mother did not travel much, her first home after she was married had a Chinese mural on the living room wall. My earliest baby pictures show me sleeping in a bassinet beneath that Chinese mural.

I would love to have that mural now that I have my own children from China. The connection is like some mystical ancestral cord that binds us. Some things in life are clearly meant to be.

All adopted children, regardless of their country of origin, have two families, two cultures. Within the United States, from state to state, the matter of culture may be of less importance. When adopting children of other cultures—from China, Haiti, South America, Africa, and so on—parents may want to be prepared to help their child or children with their dual heritage.

Children who face the prospect of exploring their birth heritage from the safety, security, and acceptance of their adopted family have potentially fewer emotional risks. Certainly a sense of belonging is one of life's most basic needs, and there are many facets to a child's adjustment to his or her new culture. Linda Lin, China Program Coordinator with Wide Horizons for Children, America's third largest adoption agency, points out that adopted children "are in the unique position of learning two cultures. Able to bridge both cultures, they serve as messengers between the two."

Put together a treasure box of items associated with the adoption. Include such things as the outfit the child was wearing, toys the child played with, airplane ticket stubs, leftover foreign currency, and memorabilia associated with the trip.

Because of this, adopted children and their families tend to learn the good things of each culture, Linda adds. It is one of the many blessings and benefits of adoption.

Adoptive parents can help provide a smooth transition into their new family by showing their children that they have an important place in their adoptive family's lineage. Because the sense of belonging is so crucial to adopted children, the reinforcement of family love is essential. One way to make an adopted child feel like a member of a new family as well as of a new culture is to give the child something representative of the family's background.

Elizabeth Wessen, an adoptive mother of Norwegian descent, received a handmade dress and sweater knitted by cousins from Norway to welcome her Chinese daughter into the family. The gesture represented a very personal way of intertwining two cultures into one family.

"It was my cousins' way of making my daughter Jia feel welcome in our family even though she came from a different culture," Beth says. "I'll always cherish the outfit and the gesture. It meant they had accepted Jia completely."

Her cousins also sent a traditional working day dress known as a *hverdags*. The dress includes a striped jumper top and dirndl skirt with a blouse that is worn under it as well as a pair of buckled shoes. The gift included a traditional pin featuring metal disks that dangle and reflect light made by another cousin to complete the ensemble.

"It had so much more meaning because it came without my asking," Beth says. "My cousins were giving Jia their history and traditions."

There are many ways parents can help their children understand and appreciate their dual adoptive and biological heritage. In doing so they must also decide to what degree their child expresses curiosity about his or her heritage and also to what degree they feel comfortable opening that particular door for their child. Personalizing the child's introduction to his or her country of origin will make the experience more significant as well as more memorable.

Keep a scrapbook with clippings about the country and its culture or events that occurred at the time of your visit or while you were waiting for the adoption to go through. You might also create a scrapbook with information about cultural traditions. Your scrapbook could also include clippings from magazines, newspapers, and educational publications as well as school projects completed by other family members relating to the birth country.

Read aloud *I Love You Like Crazy Cakes* by Rose Lewis or *Tell Me Again About the Night I Was Born* by Jamie Lee Curtis—two heartwarming books

Many families who have adopted children from Korea celebrate the day they received their new children. To recognize those special days when their children were little, parents give their children *hanboks*, or Korean ceremonial dress.

When Ed and Karen Dihrberg first adopted two children from Russia, they spoke Russian at home. Karen eagerly tried Russian recipes although she soon learned that the children preferred American foods, especially hot dogs.

Nevertheless, they try to keep their children in touch with the culture into which they were born. While in Russia they purchased several books of Russian fairy tales with divided pages that feature text in both English and Russian.

Listen to music from your child's birth country or watch a movie that shows the landscape or folk dress of your child's country of origin.

Similarly, Daniel and Linda Hardman enjoy sharing Haitian music with their three adopted children from Haiti, as well as with their other children.

Many adoption agencies hold a culture camp or other activity to keep children who have been adopted internationally in touch with the country of their birth. Often children learn about language, cultural traditions, food, crafts, and other aspects of the foreign culture. Such an introduction at the right time can be a springboard for a trip to the birth country if the child is receptive.

A child's cultural heritage might spill over into academic life as well. My daughter's day care center featured an International Month in which each classroom made decorations representing a different country. My daughter's class happened to have China. From that activity we added panda masks and Chinese fans to her collection of memorabilia from her childhood.

Jo Ann Ferguson says that she has always given her two children opportunities to acknowledge their background as adopted Korean-born Americans. A couple of years ago her family was asked to participate in the Christmas Eve Advent candle service. Each week a different family lit the candles and shared something connected with the Bible verse of the week. The Ferguson's verse had to do with traveling, specifically with reference to Mary and Joseph journeying to Bethlehem, a town where they were strangers.

Jo Ann's son only wanted to light the candles, but Jo Ann and her daughter Marianne together wrote a short piece about how Marianne had also traveled to a strange city and found a family as Mary and Joseph had.

"It was only a page long," Jo Ann says, "but when she read it there wasn't a dry eye in the church. I could see that she was proud of herself not only for writing it and reading it in front of the congregation, but also because she was proud of her story."

Angela Healy, an Irish immigrant now living in the United States, is confronted regularly with cultural issues. As the mother of an adopted daughter from China, Angela understands the issues her daughter, Olanne, will face as she grows older.

"What I wish to instill in Olanne's heart is a sense of pride in being a Healy and the deep feeling of belonging to the family for better or worse," she says. "This confidence of having an anchor is a tradition I want to impart to Olanne."

Many parents have found Beth O'Malley's books, such as *LifeBooks: Creating a Treasure for the Adopted Child* (Adoption-Works, 2000), very helpful in putting together a record of their adopted child's life.

All children find and choose their own identity, sometimes independently of their parents. Even so, family influence often determines to a great extent the person a child turns out to be, making cultural identity less significant than family identity.

My daughters will inherit my cultural traditions as well as my husband's. Those traditions have little to do with China because

Chinese customs were not part of our past. Our growing-up years were rooted in American and European customs. The traditions they inherit from us will be vital to their sense of identity because those traditions represent their family. To be associated with a family is life's strongest connection.

Some adoption organizations sponsor monthly meetings for parents to discuss their experiences with other parents of adopted children. Look for organizations in your area or look online for discussion groups.

Appendixes

Appendix A

Websites by State

Alabama

www.archives.state.al.us/kidspage/kids.html
www.earlyworks.com
www.sos.state.al.us/kidsplace/intro.htm

Alaska

www.mms.gov/alaska/kids/
www.state.ak.us/local/wildvids.html
www.state.ak.us/local/akpages/FISH.GAME/geninfo/kids/kids.htm

Arizona

www.governor.state.az.us/global/az_kids.htm
www.azrvparks.com/kids.html

Arkansas

www.arkansaskids.com/

California

www.dre.ca.gov/kidlinks.htm
www.dre.ca.gov/kids_sub.htm
www.assembly.ca.gov/kids/kids1/kids1.htm

Colorado

www.coloradokids.com/
www.colokids.com/
www.wowmuseum.com/
www.state.co.us/kids/index.html
www.rootsweb.com/~cokids/

Connecticut
www.kids.state.ct.us/

Delaware
www.hsd.org

District of Columbia
http://kids.dc.gov/

Florida
http://dhr.dos.state.fl.us/kids/index.html

Georgia
www.perryga.org/kids.php

Hawaii
www.hawaii.gov/dlnr/dofaw/kids/

Idaho
www.idahoptv.org/kids/index.html
www.accessidaho.org/education/kids.html
www2.state.id.us/gov/fyi/kidbook/index.htm

Illinois
www.state.il.us/kids/
www.illinois.gov/visiting/historic.cfm

Indiana
www.in.gov/sic/kids/
www.inspire.net/indkids.html

Iowa
www.state.ia.us/main/addressbooks/ADkids/

Kansas
www.kshs.org/kids/

Kentucky
www.gocampingamerica.com/kidspages/states/kentucky.html

Louisiana
www.gov.state.la.us/kids/default.htm

Maine
www.state.me.us/sos/kids/

Maryland
www.mdisfun.org/kids/default.asp

Massachusetts
www.state.ma.us/sec/cis/ciskid/kididx.htm

Michigan
www.michigan.gov/mikids

Minnesota
www.state.mn.us

Mississippi
www.wildlifemiss.org/kids/

Missouri
www.gov.state.mo.us/kids/

Montana
www.montanakids.com/

Nebraska
www.unicam.state.ne.us/kids/index.htm

Nevada
http://dmla.clan.lib.nv.us/docs/kids/
www.clan.lib.nv.us/polpac/library/clan/clan-kids.htm
http://webmaster.state.nv.us/kids.htm

New Hampshire
www.gencourt.state.nh.us/senate/misc/kids.html

New Jersey
www.njleg.state.nj.us/kids/index.asp
www.state.nj.us/hangout_nj/

New Mexico
www.state.nm.us/category/aboutnm/fastfacts.html

New York
www.dos.state.ny.us/kidsroom/nysfacts/factmenu.html
http://assembly.state.ny.us/kids/

North Carolina
www.secretary.state.nc.us/kidspg/homepage.asp
www.ncgov.com/asp/subpages/kidspage.asp

North Dakota
http://discovernd.com/kidzone/

Ohio
www.oplin.lib.oh.us/products/oks/

Oklahoma
www.otrd.state.ok.us/StudentGuide/

Oregon
http://bluebook.state.or.us/kids/kids.htm
www.dfw.state.or.us/springfield/kidsonly.html

Pennsylvania

http://sites.state.pa.us/kids/
www.dcnr.state.pa.us/stateparks/kids/index.htm.

Rhode Island

www.rilin.state.ri.us/studteaguide/teaguide.html
www.ri.net/schools/Central_Falls/ch/heazak/rilinks.html
www.gocampingamerica.com/kidspages/states/rhode_island.html

South Carolina

www.lpitr.state.sc.us/html-pages/student.html

South Dakota

www.state.sd.us/denr/dfta/watershedprotection/kidspage.htm
www.state.sd.us/governor/Kids/index.htm
http://kidzone.travelsd.com/index.asp

Tennessee

www.state.tn.us/governor/kidspage.htm

Texas

www.senate.state.tx.us/kids/
www.state.tx.us/category.jsp?language=eng&categoryId=1.5

Utah

www.utah.gov/learning/kidspage.html

Vermont

http://vermont.gov
www.vermont.gov/find-facts/kidspage.html

Virginia

http://legis.state.va.us/CapitolClassroom/CapitolClassroom-Home.htm
www.kidscommonwealth.virginia.gov/FunAndGames/

Washington

http://access.wa.gov/kids/
www.leg.wa.gov/common/kids/default.htm

West Virginia

www.legis.state.wv.us/kids/kids.html
www.state.wv.us

Wisconsin

www.doj.state.wi.us/kidspage/

Wyoming

www.state.wy.us/kids.asp
www.wyoming4kids.org

Appendix B

Websites Just for Kids

Children's Websites

http://home.earthlink.net/~howardorjeff/instruct.htm
www.geocities.com/EnchantedForest/5283/genekids.htm
www.rootsweb.com/~wgwkids/
www.win.org/library/services/lhgen/kidhome.html
www.genealogyspot.com/features/kids.htm
http://genealogytoday.com/junior/
www.genealogytoday.com/columns/everyday/020406.html
www.ericit.org/weblinks/weblinks.shtml

History Mystery

http://teacher.scholastic.com/histmyst/index.asp

You Be the Historian

http://americanhistory.si.edu/hohr/springer/index.htm

Walk Through Time

www.bbc.co.uk/history/walk/

Step Into Places

www.stepintoplaces.com/Resource%20Guide/Quick/Guide_DE.htm

Appendix C

Resources for Parents

Beller, Susan Provost. *Roots for Kids: A Genealogy Guide for Young People.* Baltimore: GPC, 1997.

Covert, James T., Ph.D., and Jan S. Smith, Ph.D. *Memory Makers: More Than 100 Just-for-Fun Ways to Give Children Memories to Last a Lifetime.* Portland, Oreg: Frank Amato Publications, 1988.

Eichholz, Alice. ed. *Ancestry's Red Book: American State, County & Town Sources, Rev. ed.* Salt Lake City, Utah: Ancestry, 1992.

Frisch, Karen. *Unlocking the Secrets in Old Photographs.* Salt Lake City: Ancestry, 1991.

Hudson, Gail E. "'Tis the Season for Tradition." *Child* (December/January 2000): 62–64, 66.

Krasner-Khait, Barbara. "Getting Kids Hooked on Genealogy." *Genealogical Computing.* 23, no. 1 (July–August–September 2003): 11–14.

Morgan, George G. *Your Family Reunion: How to Plan It, Organize It, and Enjoy It.* Provo, Utah: Ancestry, 2001.

MyFamily.com. *Celebrating the Family: Finding Your Place in Family History.* Friedman/Fairfax, 2002.

Szucs, Loretto Dennis and Sandra Hargreaves Luebking. *The Source: A Guidebook of American Genealogy, Rev. ed.* Salt Lake City, Utah: Ancestry, 1997.

Wagner, Edith. *The Family Reunion Sourcebook.* Los Angeles: Lowell House, 1999.

Warren, James W., and Paula Stuart Warren. *Getting the Most Mileage from Genealogical Research Trips,* Second Edition. St. Paul, Minn.: Warren Research & Marketing, 1998.

Willard, Jim and Terry. *Ancestors: A Beginner's Guide to Family History and Genealogy.* New York: Houghton Mifflin, 1997.

Wisdom, Emma J. *A Practical Guide to Planning a Family Reunion.* Nashville: Post Oak Publications, 1988.

Appendix D

Children's Books

This list of children's books is by no means comprehensive. It is intended only to represent a sample of children's books on the market with historical or genealogical orientation. Other resources you might consider are *Cobblestone,* the American history magazine for children; Scholastic Books' "Dear America" series; and Aladdin's Childhood of Famous Americans series, which include books on Abigail Adams, Davy Crockett, Thomas Edison, Abraham Lincoln, George Washington, and others.

Adoption

Creech, Sharon. *The Wanderer*. Harper Trophy, 2002.

Curtis, Jamie Lee. *Tell Me Again about the Night I Was Born.* New York: HarperCollins, 1996.

Lewis, Rose. *I Love You Like Crazy Cakes.* Boston: Little, Brown & Co., 2000.

Turner, Ann Warren. *Through Moon and Stars and Night Skies.* Harper Trophy, 1992.

Genealogy

Ayres, Katherine. *Family Tree.* Dell Yearling, 1996.

Hearne, Betsy. *Seven Brave Women.* Greenwillow, 1997.

Nixon, Joan Lowery. *Search for the Shadowman.* Yearling Books, 1998.

Shelby, Anne. *Homeplace.* Orchard Books, 2000.

History

Blos, Joan W. *A Gathering of Days: A New England Girl's Journal, 1830–1832.* New York: Aladdin Books, 1982.

Brenner, Martha. *Abe Lincoln's Hat.* New York: Scholastic, 1994.

Krupinski, Loretta. *Celia's Island Journal.* Boston: Little, Brown & Co., 1992.

Maynard, Christopher. *Incredible Words and Pictures: Knight and Castle.* London: Dorling Kindersley, 1994.

Murphy, Frank. *George Washington and the General's Dog.* New York: Random House, 2002.

Rice, Chris and Melanie. *How Children Lived: A First Book of History.* London: Dorling Kindersley, 1995.

Roop, Connie and Thomas B. Allen. *Good-bye for Today: The Diary of a Young Girl at Sea.* Atheneum. 2000.

—— and Gwen Connelly. *Let's Celebrate Thanksgiving.* Brookfield, Conn.: Millbrook, 1999.

Immigration

Bierman, Carol, and Laurie McGaw. *Journey to Ellis Island.* Hyperion, 1998.

Hest, Amy. *When Jessie Came across the Sea.* Cambridge, Mass.: Candlewick, 1997.

Tarbescu, Edith. *Annushku's Voyage.* Clarion Books, 1998.

Appendix E

Websites for Families with Adopted Children

www.connectforkids.org

The Connect for Kids website features topics of interest to adoptive parents including helping siblings adjust to a newly adopted child, keeping cultural connections alive, finding homes for teenagers, and adopting domestically. The homepage lists topics A–Z where you can find adoption, cultural connections, and others.

www.olderchildadoption.com

In the parenting section are several good articles on various topics. One article describes how to create culture camps to help internationally adopted children learn about their culture. Another article addresses the concerns of grandparents of older adopted children. You'll find one that offers suggestions for parents on helping adopted children to make the adjustment from institutionalized living to life at home.

www.storyarts.org

Story Arts Online is devoted to all aspects of storytelling including in the classroom. It offers lesson plans, activities, and a curriculum ideas exchange. Storytelling in the classroom focuses on stories as a way for children to discover their identity as people in a subculture.

www.kidsculturecenter.com

Designed for families of international adoption, this page offers customs, traditions, and celebrations in countries around the world. It includes links to events, products, and resources. This "What You Need to Know About Adoption" website offers advice and guidance on all aspects of adoption.

www.adoptivefamilytravel.com/culture_camps.html

The Ties Program offers information about various culture camps as preparation for travel to the birth country. Colorado Heritage Camp annually sponsors culture camps for children of African-American, East Indian, Korean, Russian, Chinese, Filipino, Latin American, and Vietnamese ancestry. A listing of dates and locations is included.

The culture camp program offers the opportunity for international adoptees to share common experiences and learn about the culture, traditions, and history of their birth countries.

http://adoption.about.com/library

This site offers articles on a variety of topics relating to adoption, including language, media, and reunion.

www.adoptivefamilies.com

A national magazine, *Adoptive Families,* is for parents before, during, and after adoption. It offers insights into heritage, culture shock, parental roles, and more.

Index

About the Author

Karen Frisch first became interested in genealogy as a child when her grandmother gave her a collection of old photographs from Scotland. Her interest continued to grow as she taught her high school students to combine elements of genealogical research with research projects, such as interviewing grandparents and searching through public records in northern Rhode Island. Her first book, *Unlocking the Secrets in Old Photographs*, was published by Ancestry in 1991.

With the adoption of her two daughters, Karen made two discoveries: first, that her daughters needed to grow up with a sense of belonging to their new family, and second, there was nothing on the market to help parents teach their children how to do this. Her research led her to write *Creating Junior Genealogists: Tips and Activities for Family History Fun*.

A devoted mother, genealogist, writer and teacher, Karen lives in Rhode Island with her husband, their two daughters, and their dog.